Evelyn E. Peterson

Won at MNA Convention
in Rochester, Minn.
1986   Oct. 26-29
Focus on the Future

# HORSE RACING PRIMER

# HORSE RACING PRIMER

## By Steve Davidowitz
### Horse Racing Columnist

Cover Illustration / James D. Freitag
Design / Michael A. Carroll
Composition Analyst / Brian Cravens
Copy editing / Bud Armstrong,
Mike Pashalek, Arnie Robbins,
Graydon Royce, Jim Smith.

**First printing**

***Dedication:*** For Brad, a good son, a good friend.

### Acknowledgements:

Thanks to the Daily Racing Form for permission to use their copyrighted result charts and past performance profiles and thanks to all the editors on the sports desk of the Minneapolis Star and Tribune who contributed to the success of the Primer series.

# Introduction:

With the advent of Minnesota's first racetrack, many people are seeking good information about thoroughbred racing. This book is designed to satisfy that need.

It is a compilation of columns on racing that appeared twice weekly in the Minneapolis Star and Tribune from Nov. 18, 1984, to April 28, 1985. It is intended for the novice fan and for those seeking new clues into a wonderfully diverse, intellectually challenging sport.

It contains information about breeding, racing, training, betting and every other facet of the game. It traces the history of the thoroughbred back to its roots in 17th century England, through to the prep races for the 1985 Triple Crown. It recounts some of the sport's most glorious and most embarrassing moments and it shares personal anecdotes and insights taken from 22 years of racetrack experience.

Thoroughbred racing is more than 10 or 12 horses dashing to the finish line. It is a newly born colt, bred to race with the wind. It is the craggy face of 71-year-old Woody Stephens, a horse trainer who wants to win another Derby, another Belmont Stakes. It is Panamanian-born jockey Laffit Pincay Jr., never giving up, riding a seemingly beaten horse to a desperate victory in an important race; it is Secretariat setting new standards for horse performance that may last to the end of the century.

Racing is as old as Saratoga and as new as Canterbury Downs. Writing about it for a living is one of the most exciting, most rewarding occupations in the world. Every day there are new insights, new lessons that transcend mere fun and games.

Producing and reviewing the columns that went into this book was a great deal of fun. It rekindled numerous memories and continually reinforced the reasons why someone might choose to be a racing writer. There is much to share, much to learn and the two things are one in the same.

I hope you enjoy my work and I hope it helps your game.
**Sincerely,**
**Steve Davidowitz**

# Contents

# Who, what, where, when, why and how

What exactly is a thoroughbred racehorse? How fast can they run?

How important is the jockey, the trainer or the track condition? What is turf racing? Why is there so much money in the sport? Is the game on the square? What about drugs? What's the difference between a win and a show bet, or an exacta and a daily double? Is it possible to beat the game? Are the horses treated well?

These are only a few of the questions people ask about thoroughbred racing, Minnesota's newest sport, a sport in which the grandstand spectator is as much a participant as the horse.

You will be able to find answers to these and other questions in this special series of columns. The series has one goal above all others: To provide the novice racing fan with enough information to understand and enjoy a truly fascinating sport.

Before we proceed, I should like to share some personal background and to offer a few comments about the role of a newspaper in covering pari-mutuel racing, especially a new racing situation such as we have in Minnesota.

During the last 22 years, I have spent more than 2,000 days at racetracks from Canada to California. I have seen races at 49 tracks in Florida, New Jersey, Pennsylvania, New York and 15 other states. I have watched, bet on and written about the cheapest racing in America and have had the privilege of seeing Secretariat, Seattle Slew and Affirmed win the Kentucky Derby, Preakness and Belmont Stakes. I have written a book, edited a magazine, reported on racing in various newspapers for 15 years. Through all of that, I have tried to improve the flow of information to the racing fan. It is a sad commentary on the way some states supervise the sport that the fan is seldom provided normal creature comforts, or information he deserves.

In Maryland and Pennsylvania, for instance, some of the tracks have all the ambience of a smoky poolroom and the fan is denied accurate workout information, among other failures in communication.

In California, where the tracks are first-rate and the fan is treated with respect, there still are problems, mostly connected to drugs. In California, horses are allowed to race on the Butazolidin and Lasix, but the information is not properly revealed to the betting public. This kind of callous treatment is terribly frustrating to informed racing fans who know that a horse often runs better when it is treated with those drugs. Happily, California is beginning to see the light; information about drugs is soon to be released. But it took a lot of work by a lot of racing writers to change things.

In Minnesota, we expect something different. We hope such blind spots will be few in number. New rules are being written, a track is being built and every opportunity to inform the public has to be the first order of business all the way down the line. But this is not going to be easy. The public's lack of racing knowledge must be taken seriously by every racing commissioner and track official. It is the responsibility of a good newspaper to be a a fundamental part of this mix.

The racing writer for the Star and Tribune is not the publicity department for Canterbury Downs. My job is not to promote the track, nor to overlook its shortcomings. My job is to report, comment and share insights; to educate, to keep you informed. An informed, educated public is an essential ingredient in the proper conduct of the sport.

The sport of thoroughbred racing is far more intricate than it appears to the uninitiated. Its history goes back several centuries and it has become a multibillion-dollar industry, vital to the economic well-being of several states.

Consider last fall's inaugural running of the Breeders' Cup.

Every horse in the seven races was a registered thoroughbred, tracing its roots to three horses brought to the British isles from the Arabian peninsula in the 16th century. These bloodlines have been protected and cultivated to produce a creature of magnificent bearing and speed. In today's marketplace, the best of them costs millions of dollars.

On Breeders' Cup day, $10 million in purses was distributed and $11 million was bet by 64,500 people in attendance. NBC paid almost $2 million for the broadcast rights and the signal was beamed to more than 50 countries. California earned about $600,000 in pari-mutuel taxes and millions more in tourism. Hollywood Park spent nearly $30 million on improvements to coincide with becoming the host track and jockey Angel Cordero Jr. earned about $130,000 as his share of the $1.3 million in purses he won.

High above the track, 450 reporters wrote millions of words for readers around the globe and three stewards looked at tapes to adjudicate disputes that resulted in two disqualifications worth $4 million in purses.

There were 14 American tracks and betting outlets that offered Breeders' betting, with more than 300,000 players participating in the action coast to coast.

All this came on a single racing day, the richest in racing history. But throughout the year, at tracks from New York to California, there always are big-money races and thousands of people interested in playing them. Indeed, for the last 44 years, racing has been no worse than the No. 2 spectator sport in America and it has been No. 1 in 41 of those years.

When Canterbury Downs opens, thousands of people from all walks of life will be there, many to see the first horse race of their lives. Most will be curious to see the new game in town and some will be better informed than others. This series is designed to share as much knowledge as possible.

# The sport of kings and queens

The earliest history of the thoroughbred racehorse traces back to the middle ages, when King Henry I bought an Arabian stallion and bred it to a band of British mares. The result was a faster breed of horse, one more suited to mobile warfare, one that encouraged races by knights and lords.

What followed was the birth of thoroughbred racing and a history that includes some facts so obscure they might not make it into a Trivial Pursuit game for several more centuries. People who are fascinated by this subject should consider reading "Frank Menke's Encyclopedia of Sports," first published in 1944, and William P. Robertson's "History of Thoroughbred Racing," in 1968. Both were used to prepare several columns in this series.

According to most historians, the first public racecourse was the Smithfield Track in London, built in 1174. It must have been a jolly good show because the popularity of horse races spread to dozens of county fairs throughout the British countryside.

In 1512, the first racing trophy was fashioned out of wood, a hand-carved ball decorated with flowers. By 1540, the ball was being made out of silver and 70 years later the idea for win, place and show was born — by accident. It seems a silversmith in charge of making a silver ball failed miserably, twice. The sheriff of Chester didn't know what to do with these two odd-shaped items, so he gave them away to the second and third finishers.

A century later, Queen Anne originated the *sweepstakes,* which involves a cash investment and a reward for a winning race. This was one of many advances put forth by Anne, the unheralded

4

mother of modern thoroughbred racing.

In 1703, Anne put up a $20 silver plate for a trophy for a big race at Doncaster, which had become the racing ground for the wealthiest barons and lords. In 1710, she upped the ante to a $300 gold cup and fixed the rules for competition. Races were restricted to six horses, each to carry 168 pounds, including the rider, at a distance of 4 miles per heat. This formalization of racing rules contributed a great deal to Queen Anne's popularity with her feudal allies and so did the valuable trophies she put up for the races.

In 1714, it dawned on the good queen that she was giving away the family jewels piece by piece, so she came upon a novel idea, one that has since become the foundation for the world's most important races.

Instead of merely putting up the trophy, then worth about $500, enough to feed a large family for life, the queen added a twist to the rules. All owners had to pay an entry fee of 10 guineas ($50), with the winner to take all.

Not too surprisingly, the queen's own horse, Star, won the first race under the new rules and became the first sweepstakes winner in racing history.

Queen Anne also was responsible for standardizing rules concerning racehorse breeding. She recognized the need to keep the fastest bloodstock intact, not to dilute it by breeding to slower horses. She coined the word "thoroughbred" and applied it to horses tracing their roots back to Arabian bloodlines.

Arabian horses had been the envy of cavaliers on European battlegrounds and after Queen Anne permitted a few to be bred to horses of British blood, the queen wanted to see the thoroughbred lineage kept intact. Unfortunately, her idea did not catch on until 60 years after her death.

"The English Stud Book," published for the first time in 1791 as a service to the growing list of English horse breeders, rediscovered Queen Anne's idea. A panel of British lords decided to list the top horses in training and in so doing noticed that they all traced back to three Arabian stallions imported to Britain in the mid-1600s.

The three top horses of contemporary 18th century racing were **Herod, Matchem** and **Eclipse.**

Matchem was traced back to the **Godolphin Arabian**, Herod to the **Byerly Turk** and Eclipse to **Darley's Arabian**. Godolphin, Byerly and Darley were the three men who happened to import those three Arabian horses.

Today, all thoroughbred racehorses trace back to those three Arabian stallions and the racehorse Eclipse is honored by the Eclipse Awards, given annually to the best horses in North America.

But back in the late 1700s, the fledgling thoroughbred breeding industry faced a money crunch right from the first.

For humane reasons, horses below the age of 5 were barred from competition. Most races were set at 4 miles, each requiring two, sometimes three heats on a single afternoon — too strenuous for a young horse. Even in those days it cost a lot to keep a racehorse in oats and hay, especially one that could not begin to earn its keep for five full years.

A horse breeder from St. Leger solved racing's first crisis in 1776. The breeders set up races at Doncaster for 3-year-old horses at 2 miles, one heat to decide. The inaugural race lacked an official name, but in 1777 it became known as the St. Leger Stakes, the oldest horse race in the world. To this day it is run at the same racecourse, although today it is contested at 1¾ miles.

In 1779, still another English horseman made his contribution to thoroughbred racing.

The earl of Darby, seeking to create a race for 3-year-old fillies, set up a 1½-mile race on the rolling fields of his estate at Epsom. The earl named the event the Epsom Oaks. The following year, he set up another 1½-mile race for 3-year-olds of either sex and the public labeled it "Darby's race at Epsom." Within a few runnings, and to this very day, the race became known as the Epsom Darby, (or Derby), the first derby, a forerunner to our own Kentucky Derby, an American classic that was to have its first running 105 years later.

# Early American racing 1665-1864

Horses were introduced to the Americas during the first half of the 16th century by the Spanish explorers Cortez and Coronado. Both men lost nearly all their stock and these horses became the backbone of the breed that dominated frontier life.

In 1665, New York's governor, Richard Nichols, formally set up the continent's first racecourse, on the Hempstead plains in Long Island. He named it the Newmarket course, after a famous racing ground in England. Within a decade, there also were horse races in Maryland and Virginia, but the first true thoroughbreds were not imported to America until the 18th century.

Some say the first American thoroughbred was Bully Rock in 1730, others say it was Selima in 1747, but there is no disputing the fact that by the end of the Revolutionary War, horse racing was an exceedingly popular pastime in America.

In Kentucky, numerous races were run through downtown Lexington; in New York, races were run through Greenwich Village in Manhattan; in Virginia, at least five recognized race meetings were held annually during the 1780s and '90s.

In 1788, the English thoroughbred Messenger was shipped to America and he became a remarkable sire. Not only was Messenger an outstanding thoroughbred sire, he also developed into the foundation sire for the American harness horse.

The harness horse was quick to master difficult trotting and pacing gaits, making a stunning impression pulling carts, called sulkies. It was slower than the thoroughbred, but just as graceful, and many were matched in competition at local fairs. A new racing sport was born, one with its own breeding rules, paralleling the growth of thoroughbred racing. Minnesota's own Dan Patch — unbeaten at the turn of the 20th century — was a descendant of Messenger.

In 1798, the American thoroughbred breeding industry pulled off an astonishing coup, acquiring Diomed, the winner of the inaugural running of the Epsom Derby. The price was a paltry $250, an insult to British pride, especially following the loss of Messenger, not to mention the Revolutionary War. Diomed was a landmark British racing champion, a thoroughbred with impeccable bloodlines.

Diomed's sons were mated to daughters of Messenger, the best of which was Damsel, who produced American Eclipse, the fastest horse in the world during the 1820s. At least that's what his Yankee owners claimed for him.

Forty years before the Civil War, there was no love lost between the North and the South. For many northern breeders, racing had become a full-time vocation, a pleasurable way of life. Southern breeders were jealous and some made it their patriotic duty to find a horse fast enough to take the northerners down a peg.

Col. William R. Johnson was such a southerner. In 1823, Johnson put up $10,000 to challenge American Eclipse at the Union Course on Long Island, winner take all.

More than 60,000 people showed up at the course. But on the eve of the event, scheduled for three 4-mile heats, the top southern horse went lame. Johnson offered a substitute named Henry and the northerners readily agreed. "American Eclipse is the fastest horse in the country," the northerners boasted. "No one can beat him in two out of three heats."

And they were right, to a point.

The northern champion did beat Henry in two straight heats, but only after losing the first, a disastrous result for the northern bettors. Johnson and his friends took the New York crowd for a fortune.

Knowing their horse had no chance to beat American Eclipse twice, the southerners bet everything they had on Henry to win the *first* heat. Henry raced the entire 4-mile distance at full tilt to win several hundred thousand dollars for his backers, who were perfectly willing to lose the next two heats and a mere $10,000 purse.

This group of southerners returned to the Union Course 13 years later to teach the northerners another lesson in betting strategy.

In 1836, Col. Johnson brought a horse named John Bascombe to challenge the reigning northern champion, Post Boy. This time, Johnson boasted his horse would not only win the first heat, but the second heat as well. The northern contingent, seeing a chance to get even, offered 2-1 odds to Johnson and his friends. They paid dearly for their mistake.

John Bascombe took both heats decisively, bringing Johnson and his followers a profit of nearly $2 million, a titanic sum at the time and one of the largest betting coups in racing history. (One can only wonder what might have happened to the Union if Johnson had been running the Confederacy.)

The Civil War put a premium on fast horses and dozens of thoroughbreds were imported from England during the 1860s. This in turn led to a new development in racing, the construction of full-size racetracks.

The first was Saratoga racetrack, built in upstate New York by John Morrisey in 1864. Morrisey set up a four-week August racing season, featuring stakes races for high-class horses.

Until this point, most tracks had been sparsely appointed flat racing grounds, the scene for only one or two days of racing. But Saratoga was a magnificent racing plant, with luxurious accommodations and sprawling grounds. When it opened for its first day of racing, it was one of the most beautiful racecourses in the world, a distinction that it retains today.

# Saratoga, Man o' War and the Triple Crown

After the construction of Saratoga racetrack in 1864, tracks were built in most major eastern cities, including Pimlico Racecourse in Baltimore and Churchill Downs in Louisville. The sport of horse racing was expanding into new states every year. Meetings were scheduled for three and four days per week throughout the spring and summer.

In New York, Jerome Park, named after Leonard Jerome (who was to become Winston Churchill's maternal grandfather), opened in 1866 to give New York two major tracks and the first complete racing circuit. A year later, Jerome Park was the scene for the first Belmont Stakes, at 1⅝ miles, won by the filly Ruthless.

The Belmont, which would become the final jewel in racing's Triple Crown, was run seven years before the first Preakness at Pimlico and nine years before the inaugural Kentucky Derby at Churchill Downs. These three races, the Derby, Preakness and Belmont, were patterned after the English Derby at Epsom Downs — exclusively for 3-year-old thoroughbreds — but no one thought of them as a series during the late 19th and early 20th centuries.

Breeders in New York and Maryland seldom wanted to ship their star 3-year-olds to Kentucky for the Derby. The trip across the Appalachian Mountains was quite an ordeal by riverboat and train. Nevertheless, Artistedes, the winner of the first Kentucky Derby in 1875, did run second in that year's Belmont Stakes and Algerine, third in the 1876 Preakness, won the Belmont a month later.

Four decades would pass before a Kentucky Derby winner also would win a Preakness or Belmont. In 1919, Sir Barton managed to win all three races to complete a sweep that would become one of the rarest achievements in all of sport. Yet, at the time, Sir Barton's three-race sweep hardly was noticed outside racing circles and did little to bring the Kentucky Derby's prestige up to the standard of the other two events.

Even the great Man o' War was kept out of the 1920 Kentucky Derby while he dominated his opposition in the Preakness and Belmont. Beaten as a 2-year-old by the aptly named Upset after a bad start in the Sanford Stakes, Man o' War went undefeated in 11 races as a 3-year-old, setting five American speed records.

Man o' War was the first superhorse of the 20th century, a star equal in his own way to Babe Ruth in baseball and Jim Thorpe in football and track. Throughout his 3-year-old season, Big Red, as he was called, commanded giant headlines in the newspapers while silent newsreels of his races played to packed movie houses.

To this day, some who watched all the great horses of the 20th century still rank him as the fastest thoroughbred of all time, even faster than Secretariat or Citation, both of whom were destined to be compared to Man o' War decades later. Man o' War's final career start was against 4-year-old Sir Barton in a match race for a world-record purse of $80,000. It was no contest; Man o' War beat his older rival by 20 lengths, completing an awesome racing career with record earnings of $249,465.

During the 1920s — known as the Golden Age of Sport — the Triple Crown emerged as the centerpiece of the racing season, primarily because changes were made in the format of all three races.

In 1925, the distance for the Preakness Stakes permanently was changed to 1-3/16 miles to conform to the configuration of Pimlico's new racing surface. In 1926, the Belmont distance was set at 1½ miles and the race was placed two or three weeks after the Preakness. The Kentucky Derby, which had been run at 1¼ miles since 1906, took a more direct route to improve its standing on the national racing calendar; the Derby purse was increased sharply to $70,000 in 1922, making it the richest race in the country.

This convinced Pimlico's management to increase the value of their race and to reschedule the Preakness to be run two weeks after the Derby. Although this appeared to be a concession to competition, the move was the turning point in developing the Triple Crown as we know it. The Preakness, already established as an important race, increased in prestige the moment Derby winners could appear in the Preakness field. This move also ended the possibility of a date conflict between the races. The Kentucky Derby, set for the first Saturday in May, was suddenly a natural leadoff event in a rich racing series that already included New York's Belmont Stakes.

The Belmont had been run at distances ranging from 1⅛ to 1⅝

miles throughout its first 59 years, but in 1926 it became a 1½-mile race to conform to the special configuration of the 1½-mile Belmont Park racing surface. Built with European racetracks in mind, Belmont remains the only 1½-mile track in North America.

In 1930, Gallant Fox became the second horse in racing history to win the Kentucky Derby, Preakness and Belmont and Charles Hatton, a columnist for the Morning Telegraph newspaper, called the feat a "Triple Crown Sweep." Five years later, every newspaper in the country carried the same phrase in their stories about Gallant Fox's son, Omaha, when he won all three races. Thus the value of the Kentucky Derby was magnified in the light of public acclaim for the horses that swept all three events. Indeed, under aggressive new management at Churchill Downs, the Derby would become the world's most famous horse race, the leading edge to an American institution, the Triple Crown series, an annual rite of spring.

# The fastest two minutes in sports

When Col. Matt Winn took control of Churchill Downs in 1937, he set out to make the Kentucky Derby "an American institution," the "world's most famous race."

Winn was the P.T. Barnum of thoroughbred racing, a promoter's promoter, a showman.

In 1940, Winn raised entry fees to ensure a gross purse of $100,000 for the Derby. He quadrupled the prices of all seats, invited patrons to fill the Churchill Downs infield at $2 apiece, sold mint juleps as the *official* Derby drink and sent a steady stream of Derby facts and fiction to every newspaper and radio station in the country.

As a sample of his promotional approach, Winn inflated attendance figures to 100,000 years before the race actually attracted that many fans.

Winn was nobody's fool. He knew he was selling a whole lot more than snake oil.

Derby week became a *happening,* a hustler's convention, a week of revelry, a Mardi Gras for horse people. Prices for hotels went through the roof and doubled again on Derby eve, strangely contributing to the appeal of the event. It all was born of hype and the whole state of Kentucky appeared to be in on the action. But nobody cared. A great irony was taking shape. Horseplayers journeyed to Louisville as if they were going to Mecca. And on the racetrack, the Derby was turning out to be a spectacular show.

In 1937, War Admiral, racing under stout control by jockey Charles Kurtsinger, led every step of the way to set a Derby track

13

record. Sports writer Grantland Rice called it "the fastest two minutes in sports." Joe Palmer wrote about the way the crowd greeted the horses in the post parade with a chorus of Steven Foster's "My Old Kentucky Home." Gravelly voiced Clem McCarthy broadcast the race live to millions of people glued to their living room radios coast to coast.

Racing no longer was the sport of British kings nor the sport of match races between northern breeders and southern plantation owners. Now, the Derby *was* racing and its stars were household words.

In 1938, aboard Lawrin, jockey Eddie Arcaro won his first of five Kentucky Derbies, collaborating with trainer Ben A. Jones, who would win six himself, including two Triple Crown sweeps. Arcaro, who lost the first 250 races he ever rode, would win a record 17 Triple Crown races during his 31-year career, including six in the Preakness and six in the Belmont Stakes. In his youth, however, Arcaro was a rough-and-tumble rider destined to serve a year's suspension for punching out a jockey during the running of a minor race. That incident brought back memories of a rough-house duel during the stretch run of the 1933 Kentucky Derby.

Herb Fisher was riding Head Play and Don Meade was aboard Brokers Tip. The horses were racing shoulder to shoulder down the long Churchill Downs stretch when Fisher and Meade began to fight with each other, striking out with their whips.

Meade and Brokers Tip finished first and the stewards called each jockey in on the carpet, but they didn't dare change the official result. "This is the Derby," the stewards said.

The next day's newspapers carried photographs showing Meade holding onto Fisher's saddle as the two raced to the wire, creating one of the most memorable, most controversial moments in Triple Crown history.

During the '40s, there were four more Triple Crown champions, Whirlaway, in 1941, Count Fleet in 1943, Assault in 1946 and Citation in 1948.

Whirlaway and Citation both were ridden by Arcaro, trained by Ben Jones for Calumet Farm. Citation may have been among the top two or three horses ever to race, but Whirlaway's Kentucky Derby was something out of this world.

Blocked early and forced back to last, Whirlaway uncorked a burst of speed to pass the entire field on the final turn, increasing his winning margin to eight lengths at the wire, smashing War Admiral's track record by 1-4/5 seconds.

The clockers shook their heads in disbelief. Whirlaway had run the final quarter of a mile in the unheard of time of 23-2/5 seconds. No horse except Secretariat (1973) ever has run a faster final quarter mile in the Derby, (22-4/5!) while only one other, Northern Dancer (1964), ever did it in 24 seconds flat.

Finishing the final quarter mile of a race at any distance in 24 seconds or less is extremely difficult, but it is especially difficult in races beyond a mile. (An interesting point to remember about so called stretch runners is that they do not actually pick up speed in their run to the finish line. In most cases, they just slow less noticeably than front-running types).

Such a front runner was Count Fleet, who crushed his opposition in all three 1943 Triple Crown races, winning the 1½-mile Belmont Stakes by 25 lengths, setting a track record of 2:28-1/5 in the process. Jockey Johnny Longden, who would ride more than 6,000 winners in his career as well as train 1969 Kentucky Derby winner Majestic Prince, still calls Count Fleet "the best horse in racing history." Maybe Longden is right, but he would get arguments from people who saw Citation in 1948.

After losing one race in nine tries in 1947 and a meaningless early-season sprint to the underrated Saggy, Citation won 15 straight races in 1948, at eight different tracks throughout the country. Not only did he tie Count Fleet's Belmont track record, but he won $709,470, tripling the season earnings record when there were only six $100,000 races in the United States. In today's purse structure, this would translate to approximately $4.5 million.

As the fourth Triple Crown winner in eight years, Citation made racing experts wonder if winning the Derby, Preakness and Belmont was a far easier accomplishment than it appeared. The failures of the next 25 years set the record straight.

# TV and Native Dancer, Arcaro and The Shoe

The first race I ever saw also was watched by approximately 2.5 million people. The year was 1953 and the race was the 79th Kentucky Derby — the first national telecast of an American horse race.

Native Dancer, unbeaten in 11 races, seemed a probable Triple Crown winner, a good reason to turn on the TV cameras. He was, after all, a beautifully proportioned, perfectly named grey son of Polynesian, out of the fast mare Geisha, a cinch to win the Derby.

What happened that day is preserved in the official result chart, compiled by Daily Racing Form correspondent Don Fair. The chart still produces a vivid picture, at least equal to the faded kinescopes; but I can also recall the surprise in the TV announcer's voice as he barked out longshot Dark Star's name nearing the finish. I was 11 at the time.

Here are Mr. Fair's footnotes, taken from the official result chart courtesy of Churchill Downs and the Daily Racing Form:

**Dark Star**, *alertly ridden, took command soon after the start, setting the pace to the stretch under steady rating, responded readily when set down in the drive and just lasted to withstand Native Dancer, winning with little left.* **Native Dancer**, *roughed at the first turn by Money Broker, was eased back to secure racing room, raced wide during the run to the upper turn, then saved ground entering the stretch to finish strongly, but could not overtake the winner, although probably best.*

The Derby was Native Dancer's only defeat in 22 lifetime races. He would defeat Dark Star in the Preakness and also win the Belmont Stakes. But more significantly, his electric Derby performance

16

sparked interest in every race he would run. He became a national phenomenon, a four-legged sports hero who made racing an acceptable television sport. Indeed, every Triple Crown race since 1953 has been televised throughout North America.

Coincidentally, his near miss in the Derby also typified another trend of the times; between 1949 and 1972, a period of 23 years, 15 horses would win two out of the three Triple Crown races, but none could manage a sweep of all three.

In 1955, heavily favored Nashua, trained by Sunny Jim Fitzsimmons and ridden by Eddie Arcaro, was upset in the Kentucky Derby by Swaps, who was ridden to perfection by 24-year-old William Shoemaker. But following the Derby, Swaps was shipped back to California, leaving two thirds of the Triple Crown to be won by Nashua.

In midsummer, in response to an intense letter-writing campaign conducted by an Illinois newspaper, Swaps and Nashua met on neutral ground at Washington Park in Chicago, in a 1¼-mile, $100,000 match race for the national championship. Fitzsimmons, one of the most talented horsemen in racing history, realized Swaps had a distinct speed advantage, a natural breaking ability that would make it difficult for Nashua to win. If Swaps could control the early pace, he would have an unbeatable tactical edge. Fitzsimmons countered by training Nashua to break alertly from the starting gate. He told Arcaro to go at full tilt from the outset, to surprise Shoemaker and take the lead from Swaps. That is precisely what 80,000 fans witnessed.

Shoemaker seemed unprepared for Arcaro's early tactics and the race was over before a quarter of a mile. The defeat was a rare blemish on Shoemaker's incredible 35-year career. But it was not the only blemish nor the most embarrassing.

In 1957, Shoemaker rode Gallant Man in the annual Run for the Roses, which had become the Derby's nickname. Although he would become the winningest jockey of all time, Shoemaker was destined that day to make the worst mistake in Kentucky Derby history.

Inside the final 1/16th of a mile, Shoemaker had Gallant Man in full gear, passing Bold Ruler and Federal Hill, moving to a slight lead over Iron Leige, a surprising longshot, ridden by William Hartack. Victory was imminent. But Shoemaker suddenly stood up in the saddle, apparently misjudging the finish line, a disastrous loss of concentration. Hartack seized the opportunity, pushing Iron Leige back on the lead to win the Derby by a nose.

Trainer John Nerud was so disappointed that he swore off competing in the Derby forever. Remarkably, Shoemaker overcame this embarrassing defeat to win 12 national riding championships and an astounding 8,350 races (200 plus in $100,000 stakes). But his lifetime record in the Kentucky Derby remains one of his weakest achievements, just three wins and several near misses in 24 attempts.

One of those near misses happened in 1964, when Shoemaker had his choice between the top-rated 3-year-olds in the country — Northern Dancer and Hill Rise. He chose Hill Rise; Hartack, his rival from 1957, picked up the mount on Northern Dancer.

Both horses raced head to head through the length of the Churchill Downs stretch, but it was Northern Dancer in front at the wire.

Northern Dancer then won the Preakness while Hill Rise faded to third. Finally, in the Belmont, after a gallant bid through the first 1¼ miles, Northern Dancer was defeated, finishing third to Quadrangle, a horse perfectly suited to the grueling 1½-mile distance. At the heart of this upset was a telling point about why it was becoming more difficult to sweep the Triple Crown.

Through the first half of the 20th century, winning a Triple Crown race was a coveted achievement, with a good purse attached. But in the 1950s and early 1960s, breeders were willing to pay hundreds of thousands of dollars for popular stud prospects, thus raising the value of a single win in the series. Northern Dancer was defeated because he was pressed to the limit in the Kentucky Derby and Preakness, while Quadrangle was coasting, getting his act together for the longer Belmont Stakes. Television had helped increase the desirability of such victories and a new era of escalating prices and purses had truly begun. Even so, there were few who could imagine how high these stakes eventually would go.

# Honor and dishonor/
# Kelso and Dancer's Image

During the 1960s, six colts distinguished themselves with two out of three wins in Triple Crown races: Carry Back (1961), Chateaugay (1963), Northern Dancer (1964), Kauai King (1966), Damascus (1967) and Majestic Prince (1969). All deserve serious mention in any discussion of racing history and the same is true for Buckpasser, Horse of the Year in 1966, and Dr. Fager, who won that title in 1968.

But the two most important horses of the '60s were Kelso and Dancer's Image, each for different reasons.

Kelso won five Horse of the Year titles from 1960 to 1964 to become the most honored horse in racing history. Dancer's Image lost the 1968 Kentucky Derby on a drug violation and became the most *dishonored* horse in racing history. Kelso had his nameplate etched in marble in the Hall of Fame at Saratoga. Dancer's Image had his name stripped from Churchill Downs' Wall of Champions.

As a 2-year-old in 1959, Kelso was a fractious, unmanageable colt. He raced three times at Atlantic City, winning once, finishing second twice and showing brief flashes of brilliance. Trainer Carl Hanford believed the colt might make a good Triple Crown prospect, but he gave up when Kelso injured himself in his stall twice in one month. Hanford told owner Marion Dupont Scott that Kelso needed to be gelded.

Hanford explained to Scott that gelding the colt would calm him down, that it was the only way Kelso could possibly become a good racehorse.

In the history of racing, there have been four truly great geldings — Exterminator, Forego, John Henry and Kelso, all from differ-

19

ent eras. Exterminator won the 1918 Kentucky Derby and 50 races in 100 starts. Forego won three Horse of the Year titles during the mid-70s. And John Henry, Horse of the Year in 1981 and 1984, is still going strong at age 10.

But winning five straight Horse of the Year awards is a feat that boggles the mind. Yet that's exactly what Kelso did, despite an unprecedented boom in thoroughbred breeding.

In the early 1960s, there were approximately 25,000 registered thoroughbreds born each year. The popularity of racing in the 1950s had stimulated an incredible expansion of breeding farms. The sport was in full swing at 83 tracks in 26 states and six Canadian provinces. To be king of his hill for five consecutive seasons, Kelso had to be the best of 150,000 thoroughbreds.

He won 32 stakes races, carried top weight assignments of 130 pounds or more 13 times, set or tied 13 track records and defeated Sword Dancer, Round Table, Jaipur, Gun Bow, Beau Purple, Mongo, Carry Back and Crimson Satan, champions all. In 1966, Kelso was retired with earnings of $1,977,896, a world record that would stand 14 years despite ever-increasing purses.

Kelso surely was a champion's champion, but his impact was not as great as Dancer's Image, despite the obvious difference in their abilities.

Dancer's Image was a brief shining star who had his one moment of glory taken away. But his drug disqualification from the 1968 Kentucky Derby was one of the most disturbing events in racing history.

In 1968, Phenalbutazone (Bute), an analgesic drug, was illegal in every racing state. Dancer's Image was a highly regarded Derby contender, but he was showing signs of wear as the race approached.

A dose of Bute was given about two days before the big race. Trainer Lou Cavalaris Jr. believed the drug would pass through the horse's system, but he knew he was cutting the issue close. Dancer's Image needed a final workout the day before the Derby and Cavalaris believed that the colt would not stand up to it without the drug.

Traces of the drug showed up in the postrace urinalysis, nullifying Dancer's Image victory in the world's most famous race. Three days after the race, the Churchill Downs stewards disqualified the colt, promoting second-place finisher Forward Pass to first.

Owner Peter Fuller was furious. He blamed the Kentucky State Racing Commission for failing to have an adequate drug test and he sued them to return the Derby purse and clear his horse's name.

The court battle lasted for nearly three years, until the U.S. Supreme Court sided with the state of Kentucky's decision to disqualify Dancer's Image. But the result of that final hearing probably was sealed two weeks after the Derby, in the Preakness Stakes.

Racing without aid of any pain-killing medication, Dancer's Image ran a courageous but erratic race. In the upper stretch, he suddenly veered in, then out, then in again, causing interference with Nodouble as they battled for third, while Forward Pass led the field from start to finish.

The controversial colt was racing sorely; he was having difficulty keeping a straight course. The implication was obvious: Dancer's Image must have needed medical help to win the Derby. At the very least, he clearly was sore in the Preakness and never was raced again.

Ironically, this controversy opened the door to legalized drugs for racing purposes. Veterinarians argued in favor of using Bute for its medicinal value and horsemen wanted it so they could continue to race horses with minor injuries rather than lay them up for extended vacations.

These arguments were persuasive to dozens of racing commissions, including Kentucky. Within 10 years, Bute was made legal in every racing state, except New York and Arkansas, providing it was used under veterinary supervision, with specific limits allowed in the postrace urinalysis.

In Minnesota, Bute will be legal under similar guidelines, with use barred within 24 hours of race day. Should a positive urinalysis turn up, the trainer will be held responsible, with a probable fine for a first offense or second offense and a 30-day suspension for a third.

In the Dancer's Image case, Cavalaris, the trainer, was given a 60-day suspension for the first violation of his career and Fuller, the owner, lost the most coveted victory in all of racing. For Fuller, the pain still lingers. For racing, nothing has ever been the same.

# Stretching the limits of horse performance

He was born in the spring of 1970, at the Meadow Stable Farm in Virginia, a beautiful bay colt, by Bold Ruler out of Somethingroyal by champion sire Princequillo. Bold Ruler, the proud property of Claiborne Farm of Kentucky, was the leading North American sire for seven straight seasons, beginning in 1963; Somethingroyal was the mother of six major stakes winners in a dozen breeding seasons.

This was the second mating between these royally bred thoroughbreds, but the two foals proved to be worlds apart in ability.

Claiborne *won* the coin toss for the first foal and got The Bride, a filly who couldn't outrun a fat man on a downhill slide. Meadow Stable had to wait two years for the second foal. It turned out to be Secretariat, possibly the most talented colt in racing history.

Secretariat was the only horse ever voted Horse of the Year at the age of 2.

In the Sanford Stakes at Saratoga, he overcame serious interference in the upper stretch to overtake unbeaten Chief with speed to spare. In the Hopeful, 10 days later, he went from last to first on the final turn, a move timed in 21-2/5 seconds, to win as his rider pleased.

While these and other races during Secretariat's juvenile season were among the best ever turned in by a 2-year-old, they were merely hints of the colt's awesome potential at age 3.

His Kentucky Derby, Preakness and Belmont Stakes can be studied on video tape or in the cold light of statistical comparisons and they add up to three of the greatest performances in racing history.

In the 1973 Derby, he made three distinct moves: knifing between horses on the clubhouse turn, racing outside the field in the backstretch and swinging widest of all into the stretch to beat the good horse Sham by 2½ lengths. In the process, Secretariat ran the 1¼ miles in 1:59-2/5, taking 3/5 of a second off the Derby track record while running each succeeding quarter faster than the preceding one. (His last quarter was clocked a shade under 23 seconds, by far the best final quarter mile in Triple Crown history.) No horse had ever run such a race.

In the Preakness, he circled the field on the first turn, a very risky maneuver, but the result was an identical 2½-length victory over Sham. A pair of Daily Racing Form clockers timed him in 1:53-2/5, which eclipsed the Pimlico track record by 3/5 of a second, but Secretariat was denied the mark he deserved because the official teletimer didn't run as well as he did.

In his 31-length Belmont Stakes triumph, Secretariat stretched the known limits of thoroughbred performance, cutting 2-3/5 seconds off the 16-year-old track record, setting a world record for the 1½-mile distance that still stands. The race was watched by nearly 35 million people on national television and was appreciated for other reasons. The nation was struggling with daily revelations of the Watergate scandal and Secretariat's Triple Crown sweep offered a welcome respite. He may have been just a race horse, a freak of nature at that, but he was a genuine national hero just the same.

Four years later, in a calmer political climate, Seattle Slew became a media star when he also swept the Triple Crown, the first without a defeat on his record. Unfortunately, the jet black grandson of Bold Ruler would lose his next race, an ill-advised adventure at Hollywood Park in July. But the following fall, as a 4-year-old, Seattle Slew would redeem himself, twice defeating Affirmed, the 1978 Triple Crown winner, in the only such meetings of two Triple Crown champions.

Where Seattle Slew's 1977 Triple Crown championship was achieved against modest opposition, the 1978 contest that matched Affirmed against Alydar was the most competitive ever run.

There they were, shadow to shadow, matching strides in the Belmont, completing their duel as it had begun in the Kentucky Derby. There was Steve Cauthen, the 18-year-old superstar jockey, asking Affirmed for one more ounce of energy to hold off the relentless Alydar, who was completing three of the most frustrating races in Triple Crown history.

Do race horses have any conscious awareness of competition? Do they instinctively desire to be first at the finish line? Do they know where the race ends?

Affirmed seemed to know. Every time jockey Jorge Velasquez coaxed Alydar into a higher gear, Affirmed would reply with a faster gait of his own. In the Preakness, he led the field under Cauthen's light hold on the reins and literally waited for Alydar to reach even terms with him, curling his ears backward as Alydar approached at the top of the stretch. From there, he outkicked Alydar in the fastest final 3/16 of a mile in Preakness history. Cauthen, marveling at his mount's determination, later admitted that he did absolutely nothing to get Affirmed into gear. "He did it totally on his own," he said.

Are race horses courageous?

In their stirring Belmont finale, Affirmed and Alydar were impossible to separate for the final mile. But Affirmed would not let his rival pass at the wire.

Alydar was simply one notch slower. But that did not stop him from digging in bravely in every race, trying his gut-wrenching best down to the final stride.

# In megabuck sports world, horse racing is a giant

We have traced the history of thoroughbred racing from its 17th century origins in England through the most recent winners of the American Triple Crown. We should pause a moment. Great changes are in progress. The economic realities are vastly different in the 1980s than they were a few decades ago.

In 1964, there were 46,922 races in North America with about $121 million in purses. Ten years later, there were 65,312 races with $213 million in purses. In 1984, more than $500 million was awarded in more than 70,000 races.

Suddenly we have expensive veterinary care, legalized drugs, off-track betting, multimillion-dollar stakes races, megabuck breeding contracts, the Twin Double, the Perfecta, Trifecta, Double Exacta and the Pick Six.

Jockeys ride at Belmont Park in the afternoon and at the Meadowlands at night. Top trainers supervise upward of 150 horses in four or five states. The best horses routinely are flown from New York to California for a weekend stakes.

In 1957, jockey William Hartack won a record $3.01 million in purses. Ten years later, Braulio Baeza barely broke that mark with $3.08 million. Then, in 1977, Steve Cauthen won $6.15 million, setting a record many believed would last for decades. The next year it was broken by Darrell McHargue. But the story doesn't end there. In 1984, Angel Cordero Jr., Chris McCarron and Laffit Pincay Jr. won more than $11 million apiece.

In the megabuck world of professional sports, thoroughbred racing has become a giant among pygmies, with an estimated $40 billion invested in thousands of breeding farms and allied industries. The breeding industry has become one the country's most lucrative, an industry that made record profits during the recent recession and is doing even better in the present recovery.

Last summer at the Keeneland, Ky., and Saratoga, N.Y., yearling sales, the average price for an unraced, 1-year-old thoroughbred was nearly $300,000. About 700 were sold, some to European buyers who bid by telephone while they watched the proceedings on closed-circuit TV. Five sons of Seattle Slew and Northern Dancer were sold at these auctions for $1 million to $3 million apiece.

In 1985, the winner of the Kentucky Derby was instantly worth a minimum of $8 million. And breeding experts said a sweep of the Triple Crown would have been worth $50 million.

Such fantastic sums are not paid because of a masochistic desire to lose a fortune. In the volatile world of international trade, a share of a royally bred racing champion is the safest, best investment money can buy. Consider the case of Devil's Bag, *the flop* of 1984.

As a 2-year-old, Devil's Bag was the most ballyhooed young horse since Secretariat. He was unbeaten in five swiftly run races, a son of Halo, who also had sired Sunny's Halo, the winner of the 1983 Kentucky Derby. Breeders were falling all over themselves trying to buy a piece of Devil's Bag. The colt became a media superstar, a projected Triple Crown winner. Hickory Tree Farm was virtually forced to sell a half interest, for $16 million, to protect against injury, death, or disaster.

The colt lost much of his superhorse rating when he was soundly defeated by Time for a Change and Dr. Carter in the Flamingo Stakes at Hialeah in March 1984. Although Devil's Bag did win his next three races, all against modest opposition, he was sensibly withdrawn from the Kentucky Derby when it was obvious he couldn't win. A few days after the Derby, the syndicate retired their $36 million investment to stud.

At stud, Devil's Bag is a guaranteed winner, a surefire money tree for the next four years, whether or not he will sire a single horse worth a nickel.

In 1985, Devil's Bag will service approximately 40 mares at Claiborne Farm in Paris, Ky. These breeding sessions will cost the owner of the mare approximately $175,000 apiece. In 1986, Devil's Bag will meet 40 new mares and the same for the year after that. His first yearlings will be sold at public auction in 1987.

Breeders will pay millions for the best looking sons and daughters of Devil's Bag. And they will do so again in his fourth breeding season, while he has serviced another 40 mares.

All these breeding contracts and purchase agreements will produce upward of $50 million in revenue, before a single foal competes in a race. Thus, a huge profit on the original investment is guaranteed and many millions more will be made if the colt produces good quality stock.

Consider what happened to Seattle Slew, who was syndicated for $10 million when he retired in 1978. Seattle Slew's first crop of foals hit the racetrack in 1982. Landaluce was voted an Eclipse Award as the top 2-year-old filly. Slewpy won more than $400,000 and was the fifth-leading 2-year-old colt. In 1983, Slew o' Gold was voted top 3-year-old and Swale was the second-rated juvenile behind Devil's Bag. In 1984, Swale won the Kentucky Derby and Belmont Stakes and Slew o' Gold earned a staggering $3 million in purses while winning five of six races in the summer and fall.

In November 1984, a single breeding season to Seattle Slew was sold at auction for $700,000 and the overall value of his syndicate was reappraised at $120 million. That's 12 times the original investment in less than six years.

# The state's role and responsibilities

The pari-mutuel betting system was introduced by Pierre Oller in Paris in 1865. The system was introduced to Saratoga and Churchill Downs in 1875. The primitive adding machines that were used to calculate the odds were hardly noticed; most fans preferred betting with licensed bookmakers in the grandstand betting rings.

Bookmakers paid daily rental fees and charged players a 5 percent commission for each dollar bet. The shrewdest of them maintained secret connections to leading stables in order to keep tabs on every horse on the grounds. When a highly regarded contender was reported to be off his game, the bookmaker would inflate its odds to invite more play. Likewise, there were many gamblers who knew how to play the other side of the fence.

Some were notoriously adept at putting over a well-hidden speedster at juicy odds. (Fast horses occasionally were substituted for slow ones by painting over key markings.) In those years, racing was a diabolical battle of wits involving many shady characters and the uninformed fan was at the mercy of assorted stings and scams.

A powerful reform movement was taking hold in America during this period and many states were moved to stop racing altogether. Churchill Downs and a few other tracks were permitted to remain open because they had pari-mutuel machines in place. Slowly, these machines came into favor with the betting public and many states took notice. By 1940, 20 states had reauthorized pari-mutuel wagering, while bookmakers were banned from the sport.

With these reforms, each state became a partner in the racing business, sharing in the revenue produced, establishing rules, assuming a supervisory role. This relationship has continued to this day, but not without problems.

Most politicians were taught to regard racing as fair game for abusive tax laws. Racing commissioners were chosen for their contributions to political campaigns rather than for their expertise. Pari-mutuel taxes were increased from 5 percent to 10, then 15 and 20 percent of each dollar wagered. These tax increases were made without regard to the fan or the financial stability of the tracks. The sport was seen as a golden goose, an unparalleled source of tax revenue, and there were few legislators or racing officials who saw the consequences of their actions.

In 1950, 26 states raked in nearly $100 million in pari-mutuel tax revenue during 3,300 racing days. The average rate of pari-mutuel taxation on each dollar bet was less than 13 percent.

In 1960, 27 states produced nearly $300 million in tax revenue (a 300 percent increase) during 5,000 racing days, (a 52 percent increase) and the average pari-mutuel tax was 15 percent.

By 1970, tax revenue rose to $450 million, (a 50 percent increase over 1960), while the number of racing days went up to 6,200 (a 25 percent increase). The average pari-mutuel tax was 17 percent.

Although total tax revenue and racing dates have increased sharply during the next 15 years, the sport has not been in good health. Almost 90 percent of all racetracks in the country have suffered severe losses in daily average attendance and net revenue. The sport may have been enjoying a boom in popularity, but the state has been bleeding the game dry.

To battle the trends, some tracks began to introduce new forms of wagering and requested more racing days. The states happily expanded the schedule and expanded it some more. At the same time, they also increased the overall pari-mutuel tax rates to exorbitant levels. (Most states have raised the pari-mutuel tax to 17 percent on win, place and show bets and 20 to 25 percent on each of the new wagering devices).

All these taxes have remained a part of the racing game although they have continued to threaten the health of the entire racing industry. Many tracks have, in fact, been driven out of business during the past 15 years and more will surely follow under present conditions.

Currently, the total pari-mutuel tax revenue in 30 racing states is about $675 million (from 8,500 racing dates). Golden eggs are still being produced in record numbers, but the old bird isn't smiling. A little help is long overdue.

For example, consider the amazing case of New York state, the nation's No. 1 source of pari-mutuel tax revenue.

In 1982 and 1983, while producing nearly $400 million in combined tax revenue for the state, the New York Racing Association, a nonprofit organization, had to borrow $12 million to pay its basic operating costs. In both those years, the association asked the New York Legislature to reduce the pari-mutuel tax from 17 percent to 14 percent. The association argued unsuccessfully that the reduction in tax would lead to increased attendance and increased stability for the racing industry. The association pointed out that an experimental reduction to 14 percent tried in 1978 had *increased* track attendance while holding intact state tax revenues. The New York Legislature turned down the request twice.

In 1983, pari-mutuel tax revenues declined for the first time in New York history. Within weeks after the figures became public, the Legislature panicked. A bill to reduce the tax rate to 15 percent was passed by the New York House with further changes proposed by the Senate. By mid-1985, a completely revised pari-mutuel tax code is expected to become law. Maybe there's a lesson for other states to be found in New York's turnabout, but don't count on it. Minnesota's pari-mutuel tax is set for 17 percent on win, place and show and 23 percent on daily doubles and exactas. Both of those percentages are too high, as they are in most other states.

# Basic betting rules and Murphy's Law

It's time to get into the real stuff. You know, b-e-t-t-i-n-g.

Get ready, folks. This is heavy.

You make a bet by buying a pari-mutuel ticket on the horse you think is most likely to win and you cash it when the official result says you're right. Once in a while (ha), you will see your perfectly logical choice get boxed, blocked or beaten in a photo finish just when it's about to turn your $2 investment into an island vacation.

Do you remember Murphy's Law? If something can go wrong, it will go wrong? Be forewarned. Murphy was a horseplayer and racing was where he hammered out his philosophy. What he meant to say was this: If you need to win a photo finish for $1,000, you'll probably run second. If you're going to win 20 cents, you're an absolute cinch.

Racing is a great game, a supreme intellectual challenge, a diabolical one at that. Sometimes the answer to a prerace puzzle is lodged in the back of your brain. Way back, alongside obscure facts and names like Ron VanderKelen (On Wisconsin!) or Mickey Mantle's 1957 batting average (Let me see, was it .356, .353 or .295?).

Sometimes you remember the way a particular trainer shipped in to score a victory with a well-rested horse and the man's name rings a quiet bell that doesn't go off until the starting gate opens. Of course, the trainer's horse jumps out of the gate in front of the pack. And there you are, helpless, watching that horse repulse the bid of your selection as the two duel down the stretch. A few minutes after the trainer's horse has his picture taken in the winner's circle, you look up in anguish at the prices on the tote board and see $44.40 to win, $12.60 to place, $5 to show. Your horse — the one you bet $20 to win — finished a courageous second. He gamely outdueled three stretch runners in the final 1/16th of a mile to win the photo for the place. You were thrilled to see that. So was Murphy.

All is not lost. The next time you will be programmed to remember how this trainer operates and you will go to the track after a sleepless night of study, thinking you know something that nobody else knows. You will smile quietly to yourself as the couple next to you debates the merits of two horses who don't stand a chance. You will go to the betting windows with confidence and know you've made a brilliant decision.

After the race, the couple will be seen counting their winnings on a $268.00 payoff. They just couldn't reach a clear-cut decision, they told you, so they bet *both* horses **first** and **second** in the exacta. The trainer's horse? Do you really need to ask?

Yes, the sport of kings is a great game. It's a mind-bending challenge and you just can't beat it for thrills or suspense.

Once I was on my way to the Pimlico racetrack in downtown Baltimore. It was 12:30 p.m. Post time for the first race was 1 o'clock. I was 5 minutes away, in love with a horse in the first race. He had great form, although few people could have known that, because most fans don't take the time to keep track of individual trainers and their winning patterns.

I do. And this horse was trained by a talented horsewoman, a jewel of consistency, a 25 percent lifetime winner, a woman who knew how to win a race with a horse that had not been in competition for months. When she set up a horse for a top race after a long vacation, there were telltale signs in the horse's record as it appeared in the Daily Racing Form.

Transmission trouble. My car stopped dead on the Baltimore beltway. The horse won, $12.60. Murphy's Law.

About two weeks later, as fate would have it, I was in an identical spot, about 5 minutes from Pimlico with another surefire winner in my head. This time I got there with 20 minutes to spare and bet six daily double combinations and enough to win and place to reward myself with a new typewriter.

Sorry. No typewriter. The jockey fell off in the first stride out of the gate and it didn't matter that the horse finished a length in front of the pack. When the jockey falls off, you lose. Murphy's Law.

But, as I said, it's a great game and there are things you ought to know right away.

For instance: You can lose a lot of money at the track if you think it's an easy game. And you can lose it in record time if you think you've found a foolproof system. Systems — even those built on sound concepts and painstaking research — only work for fleeting moments. Blame it on Murphy. Betting systems work perfectly while you are testing them on paper, but the moment you begin to bet serious money on them, you will lose 59 straight races.

Another first-class losing idea is to bet the public betting favorite all the time. The betting favorite wins approximately 30 percent of all races in America, a darn good percentage, but the average payoff is only $5.20. If you bet $2 per race, you can expect to cash three of every 10 plays and lose approximately $4.40 of your total $20.

Sure, some public favorites are outstanding bets, but the best winning idea I know of is to find well-qualified contenders that the crowd underestimates.

# At the racetrack,
# we make the odds

Betting at the racetrack is much different than casino betting, which pits the player against predetermined odds that always are slightly lower than the true mathematical probabilities.

In roulette, for instance, the mathematical odds against a winning spin always are 37-1 (36 numbers, plus zero and double zero), but the payoff is never that high. This means that luck is the only factor that can produce a winning day at roulette. In other words, the more often someone plays roulette, the more likely he will be busted out of the game.

Racetrack betting is no less a matter of luck for anyone who goes out for a day of blind selections based on horses' names or the colors worn by jockeys. But for those willing to learn a few skills, the sport offers a much fairer deal.

In racing, the crowd determines the odds on every horse in every race, setting up intriguing possibilities for good players.

When a racetrack crowd overbets one or more horses, the odds on such horses drop, sometimes *below* their fair value. Simultaneously, this depression causes the odds on other horses in the race to go up, sometimes *above* their fair value.

Thus, good players are mindful that racetrack betting pools perform like the stock market in reverse. A horse getting a lot of play will go to post at low odds and a horse getting very little play will go to the post at generous odds. Good players also tend to acquire skills found in other challenging games, such as poker and bridge. They learn when to bet with or against the crowd, just as good poker and bridge players learn when to press or pass a hand.

At the racetrack, there are many straightforward betting opportunities, none more often repeated than the hypothetical situation described below. To understand its implications is to see the foundation for a solid racetrack betting strategy.

The hypothetical race can be of any class level, at any distance, but its one dominant characteristic is the presence of a single front-runner. (Players learn to recognize such horses through familiarity with performance records in the Daily Racing Form. Spotting a front-runner is not difficult and we will demonstrate solid methods to do so in future articles in this series.)

In this situation, a good jockey gets the opportunity to slow the pace, permitting his front-running horse a breather, conserving its energy for the stretch run.

This principle of pace is a vital underpinning of basic handicapping, but it still produces many winners at longshot prices.

Often a stretch-runner will find favor with the crowd because last week it finished well against a similar field. (Stretch-runners actually do not pick up speed during the late stages of their races. They pace themselves naturally or do not fight the jockey when they are coaxed to accept restraint. As a result, they expend less energy than most front-runners, slowing down more gradually. They win races when front-runners waste their energy getting to the final yards.)

Maybe the crowd has bet enough money to make the fastest finisher in the race an 8-5 ($1.60 to $1.00) betting favorite. But the crowd may have made a mistake. In our hypothetical situation, the pace of today's race would be against the stretch-runner. He should not be favored; the lone front-runner is a much better bet to win.

But if we were to change the circumstances of this hypothetical race, we might be compelled to look at the same horses differently. Perhaps the front-runner is not the only speedball in the field. Maybe another fast-breaking horse is in the race, a horse capable of applying pressure from the start. In this instance, the stretch-runner would benefit from the likely duel for the lead and would deserve a much stronger winning chance. The competitition for the lead would compromise the chances of *both* front-running horses and *neither* would be able to relax at any stage of the race.

Both speedsters now would face difficult problems. Either could still win the race, especially if one was vastly superior to the other, or if the racing surface was packed down so hard that it did not tax their stamina. But under normal conditions, a speed duel between two front-runners is likely to hurt both.

A good horseplayer makes it a point to evaluate the implications of pace before settling on a selection. The reasons for this are two of the best handicapping ideas ever discovered:

■ On a relatively normal racing surface, when severe competition exists for the early lead, the horse with a finishing kick deserves an edge.

■ A lone front-running horse is always a legitimate winning threat.

In the case of a lone front-runner, a good player would be very pleased to see the crowd overbet the chances of any stretch-runner. The odds on the front-runner might go up to 4-1 or considerably higher. Sometimes the crowd might even ignore the front-runner completely. Perhaps he has a terrible win record; maybe he has never won a race. Even so, if today he is in a favorable pace situation, he could win at incredible odds.

The point is this: Race track crowds are influenced by many things, including the opinions of newspaper handicappers and other sources of information. But a good player goes his own way, relying on sound handicapping principles, taking advantage of the crowd's mistakes.

Without wishing to overstate the case, I sincerely believe a winning race track strategy can be built strictly around the basic principle of pace as spelled out above. Many other tools exist. Many other facets of the game are worth contemplating and some will be presented during this series, but, for now, just this single idea will do.

It's a winning idea, a relatively easy one, one that has been true for centuries, one that probably will be true when Canterbury Downs is 100 years old. And it can be stated simply: *Pace makes the race.*

# It's a horse,
# of course

To build a solid foundation of racing knowledge, you need to be familiar with certain terms. Not surprisingly, there are times when a picture is literally worth a thousand words.

Our glossary of racing terms begins with the conformation of the race horse.

The knee area of the rear leg is called the *hock*. The hock on the rear leg flexes differently than the knee on the front leg. This difference permits the horse to propel itself from the rear. The next time you see a film of a race, watch carefully. The horse will push off with one rear leg, then the other. For a moment, all four legs will be off the ground as the horse's front legs extend 22 to 27 feet farther down the track.

The average race horse weighs about 1,100 pounds, thus creating tremendous force in motion. All that force passes through the shoulder, the knee, the canon bone and the fetlock and lands on one of its front hoofs, followed quickly by the other hoof, followed by the rear legs again.

The front leg that stretches out farthest is called the *lead* leg and the jockey on the horse's back can instruct a well-trained horse to change leads with a slight tug of his hands on the reins. Changing leads is like downshifting gears in an automobile. The horse accelerates slightly or keeps his pace intact.

With racing experience, most thoroughbreds learn to change leads on their own as they complete a turn and head into the stretch. But some horses change leads too often, a sign of immaturity or soreness. The immature horse is racing greenly and compromising his

# Anatomy of a thoroughbred

Poll, Forelock, Neck, Forehead, Crest, Face, Withers, Loins, Back, Point of the hip, Muzzle, Jaw, Croup, Cheek, Throatlatch, Tail, Point of shoulder, Hip joint, Breast, Arm, Gaskin, or second thigh, Forearm, Ribs, Flank, Girth-place, Stifle, Knee, Elbow, Chestnut, Hock, Tendon, Cannon, Fetlock joint (ankle), Cannon bone, Coronet, Fetlock, Hoof, Pasten

chances. The sore horse is not lame but is feeling tender. He is shifting the burden of weight at the point of discomfort and is not going to maintain his best speed very long.

The conformation of a sprinting thoroughbred usually is marked by a thick hindquarters and a shorter *barrel* area, which is the area between the *shoulder* and the *point of the hip*. Sprinters are best suited to races less than one mile and some are at their best at six furlongs (three-fourths of a mile) or less. Yes, a furlong is an eighth of a mile.

Horses bred to reach peak ability beyond a mile usually have slightly elongated bodies and some have broader chests for greater lung capacity. In all cases, good conformation translates to better balance and the only way to really measure it is not when a horse is standing posed for a portrait but when it is in full stride. Occasionally, the ugly duckling in the crowd turns out to be poetry in motion.

Because of genetic laws, thoroughbred race horses come in only certain shades and colors.

Bay/ Various shades of yellowish tan to dark auburn covering the entire horse, except for the lower legs, mane and tail, which are black except when white markings are present — John Henry, for example.

Dark bay or brown/ Shades of tan and brown throughout, with large areas of tan on thighs, flanks, shoulders and head — Kelso, for example.

Black/ Black and only black, except for possible white markings on face, mane or lower legs — Seattle Slew, for example.

Chestnut/ A range of light yellow to deep liver, a golden hue, with no black on legs. Optional white markings. Secretariat, for example.

Grey/ A mixture of white and black hairs. Native Dancer, for example.

Roan/ A mixture of red and white hairs. Princess Rooney, for example.

Markings on the legs are always white. Markings on the face may be white or flesh colored. Markings on the body are usually white, but shades of black, red or brown are possible.

The male horse is a colt, until he is a 5-year-old, when he becomes a horse. The female thoroughbred is called a filly until her fifth birthday, when she becomes a mare.

A colt or horse with altered or nonfunctioning genitalia is a gelding. A colt or horse with one testicle in the proper place and the other inside his body cavity is called a ridgling. Procreation is not usually impaired for ridglings.

Speaking of procreation, Jan. 1 is more than the beginning of a new year. It is the official birthday for every race horse in the world. All foals born in 1985 become yearlings next Jan. 1, all yearlings become 2-year-olds and so on.

# Age, sex, distance and weight

🐎
_____

Jan. 1 is the universal birthday for all thoroughbreds. Foals of 1983 now are 2-year-olds and some have begun their racing careers.

In Florida, during January, 2-year-olds compete in 2- and 3-furlong dashes. These races are run without turns, through the stretch in front of the grandstand. During February, March and April, at tracks all over the country, these juvenile horses will compete at 4, 4½, 5 and 5½ furlongs. For these races, the starting gate is positioned farther back, on the turn or in the backstretch, while the finish line remains in the same place.

In the summer and fall, the distances for 2-year-old races are stretched to 6 furlongs, then to 6½, 7 and finally to a mile and longer. Through the next winter and spring, when 2-year-olds turn 3, many will remain in competition at 1 mile or less, but the best of them will compete in races at 1⅛ and longer. The Kentucky Derby, for instance, which is always run on the first Saturday in May, marks the first time 3 year-olds are asked to compete at the 1¼-mile distance. This is a prime reason why the Derby is such a difficult race to win.

Some 2-year-olds show precocious signs of ability from the first day on the track, but most acquire bad habits that inhibit their progress. It's the job of the trainer to straighten them out. Good trainers know how to harness raw speed into early-season victories, great trainers know how to take that talent and develop it, using early races as a training ground for richer events later in the year.

A 2-year-old that shows steady improvement during the late summer and fall is likely to continue to develop as the distances stretch out to 1⅛ and 1¼ miles the next spring. On the other hand, a 2-year-old bent on setting early-season track records probably will burn himself out or break down.

Breeding plays an important part in this relationship between age and racing distance. So does the training regimen.

The mating of a speed-crazy sire and dam is not likely to produce a champion distance runner. Conversely, a mating between a pair of distance specialists is not likely to produce a champion sprinter. Each offspring is bound to be handled differently by its trainer.

Two-year-olds are kept in races exclusively for 2-year-olds. Three-year-olds are given plenty of opportunities to race with their own age group as well as meet their elders.

Races for 3-year-olds and up begin in the spring, but lighter weights are always assigned to the younger horses. These weight assignments are designed to equalize things between the 3-year-old and his older rivals. The total weight includes the jockey's weight and, if needed, lead weights in the saddle pockets.

Weight is an important part of racing. It has been used as an equalizer for centuries and the official Jockey Club scale of weights offers theoretical guidelines for each age at every distance during every month of the year.

The official scale of weights also includes a female sex allowance of three or five pounds depending on the time of year. This allowance is designed to compensate for physical differences between the fillies and colts. Genuine Risk, for example, carried 121 pounds when she won the 1980 Kentucky Derby, while all the colts in the race carried 126.

Age-linked weight concessions can be just as important. If a trainer races a 3-year-old against older horses in April, May or June, he is putting his young horse against experienced, mature competition. A significant break in the weights will be needed if the 3-year-old is to have a chance.

Weight is a controversial subject. Some say it is vital to picking winners, others believe it has only limited value. I subscribe to the latter view, but my research has determined that weight is a key factor in horse performance when it is linked to age differences and distances beyond a mile. But even at such distances, a far more important factor is the horse's training regimen, including the way it was handled during the earliest days of its 2-year-old season.

If a young horse is pushed into a series of short races during the early months at 2, it is unlikely to have stamina for longer races at 3. If it is used too hard, too early in the year, it will lose its form later in the season. On the other hand, a fast 2-year-old that is given a chance to develop will have a fine chance to become a money-making thoroughbred for several seasons, perhaps even a Triple Crown contender.

Patience, timing, breeding, these are the keys to good racetrack horsemanship and for the estimated 37,000 newly-turned 2-year-old American racehorses, it all started Jan. 1. It will be interesting to follow their progress.

# Kusner, Crump and Rubin/ The first women jockeys

Kathy Kusner was the first woman to obtain a jockey's license, Diane Crump was the first to ride in a race and Barbara Jo Rubin was the first to win.

Kusner, a two-time member of the U.S. Olympic equestrian team, was denied a jockey's license by the Maryland Racing Commission (MRC) in 1968 but won a federal court appeal.

The MRC contended that women were neither physically nor emotionally equipped to compete in such a dangerous sport. Many male jockeys testified in support of that position. Kusner argued that her formal equestrian experience provided a better background for race riding than most licensed jockeys.

The court concluded Kusner's civil rights had been violated and ordered the Maryland Racing Commission to issue a provisional license, breaking new ground for women on the race track.

But Kusner, 28 at the time, never did get a chance to be the first woman to ride or win a race. A few weeks after winning her appeal, she suffered a broken leg in a spill at a Madison Square Garden horse show. Seven months later, she appeared in a few races at Laurel racecourse, but other women already had ridden and won races in Florida, West Virginia and Kentucky.

On Feb. 7, 1969, Diane Crump rode Bridle 'n Bit to a sixth-place finish at Hialeah Park. Two weeks later, Barbara Jo Rubin began a string of winning firsts with a victory aboard Cohesion at Charlestown racetrack in West Virginia. Rubin, now a free-lance artist in West Virginia, also became the first woman to win a race in Maryland and New York. (Rubin won both ends of the daily double with her first two riding assignments at Aqueduct).

Crump rode with modest success in Florida, New Jersey and Kentucky and was the first woman to ride in the Kentucky Derby, finishing 15th aboard Fathom in 1970. She is one of only two women ever to ride in a Triple Crown race. The other, Patricia Cooksey, rode So Vague to an 11th-place finish in the 1984 Kentucky Derby.

Currently, according to the National Jockey's Guild, there are about 200 women among the 1,600 licensed jockeys in the United States, a sign of remarkable progress. But none has ever made the top 20 yearly earnings list, nor do any have exclusive contracts with top stables.

Prejudice? Discrimination? Perhaps so in some cases, but most often the problem resembles a "Catch 22" situation, a dilemma women are beginning to solve.

At the root of the problem is the need for practical experience to master the art of guiding a 1,100-pound animal out of a starting gate, in traffic with other horses, while in direct competition with skilled male athletes who have more experience and inherently greater body strength. Horse racing is not pro football, nor is it as dangerous as boxing, but it isn't patty-cake either.

Until the 1980s, few women were encouraged to improve their leg and wrist strength and few prominent owners and trainers were willing to entrust expensive racing stock to women jockeys.

Nevertheless, several women, including Julie Krone, Mary Ann Alligood, Mary Russ, Lisa Ruch and Patricia Cooksey, have broken through to win important stakes.

Krone won the Atlantic City riding title in 1982 and 1983, while other women have led the standings at Arlington Park in Chicago and other tracks. In 1982, Ruch made another major breakthrough, winning the $100,000 Black Eyed Susan Stakes at Pimlico racecourse. The Black Eyed Susan is the companion filly event to the world famous Preakness Stakes.

In racing, fillies are given thousands of opportunities to compete against their own kind, but the majority of races are open to horses of both sexes, although most owners and trainers are reluctant to match their best fillies against top colts. We humans could glean a lesson or two from those fillies that got the chance.

Only twice in racing history have fillies won the Kentucky Derby — Regret in 1915 and Genuine Risk in 1980. But before we conclude that fillies are not equipped to meet and defeat colts, we should examine one aspect of the situation a little closer. Specifically, between 1959 and 1980, no filly was given the opportunity to compete in the Kentucky Derby, a fact that reflects the prevailing prejudice of the majority of American owners, breeders and trainers.

In Europe, however, especially during the last 15 years, many self-imposed restrictions against matching fillies with colts have been eliminated with interesting results. For instance, consider recent results in Europe's most prestigious thoroughbred race, L' Prix De L'Arc de Triomphe. During the last 12 runnings, seven female racehorses have posted victories, including a 1-2-3 sweep of the top positions in 1978. Moreover, the 1983 Arc winner, All Along, was shipped to America, where she promptly defeated the best male horses in Canada and the United States in three world-class events, the Man o' War Stakes, the Canadian International Championship and the Washington, D.C., International. At the end of her four-race winning romp on two continents, All Along was voted the Eclipse Award as the North American Horse of the Year.

# A new ERA for racing/ Equality has arrived

Gone are the days when women were barred from becoming jockeys, male jockeys refused to compete against women and curiosity races matched women jockeys exclusively against each other.

Today's women ride everywhere on equal terms with men, participate on all levels of racing and are among the most successful and influential members of the racing community.

There are women horse owners, breeders, writers, editors, publicists, photographers, racetrack executives, veterinarians, trainers and racing officials. Some have been in the game for decades, but most entered the sport after 1969, when Kathy Kusner, Dianne Crump and Barbara Jo Rubin made their debuts as jockeys. Here is a partial list of the most successful women in racing:

Marge Everrett, former owner of Arlington Park, is the principal owner of Hollywood Park, the host track for the inaugural running of the $10 million Breeders' Cup last November.

Mrs. Penny Chenery, owner of 1973 Triple Crown winner Secretariat and a prominent officer of the New York Racing Association, is president of the National Thoroughbred Owners and Breeders' Association.

Mrs. Marion DuPont Scott owned five-time Horse of the Year Kelso; Mrs. Stuart Janney owned Ruffian, the ill-fated filly champion of 1974 and '75; Mrs. Patricia Wolfson owned and bred the 1978 Triple Crown winner, Affirmed; Mrs. Eugene Markey owned and supervised Calumet Farm for two decades until her death three years ago, and Minnesota's Frances A. Genter has been a prominent owner of top-quality horses throughout her long association with the sport.

Joan Pew is chairwoman of the Pennsylvania State Racing Commission and treasurer of the National Association of State Racing Commissioners. There are numerous other women racing commissioners throughout the country, including four (out of nine) on the Minnesota Racing Commission: Rosemary Fruehling, Kris Sandra, Carol Connolly and Joyce Farrell.

Maryjean Wall has been the regular racing writer for the Lexington Herald for 10 years; Robin Foster served as managing editor of the prestigious Thoroughbred Record magazine until December 1984. Both publications operate in the heart of the breeding marketplace.

In 1974, Wall and freelance writer Susan McCabe were the first women admitted into the National Turf Writers Association. In 1985, there are more than 50 women members.

Sharon Smith is the Eclipse Award-winning racing commentator for ESPN television. Charlsey Cantey is the Eclipse Award-winning racing commentator for WOR-TV in New York.

Claudia Starr is the publicity director for the $10 million Breeders' Cup. Christine McLaughlin, a former publicity director at Tampa Bay Downs, now runs her own racing-oriented public relations firm. Jane Goldstein has been the publicity director at Santa Anita Park the past seven years.

Who was the first woman trainer?

The record is not conclusive, but Margaret Maclennan was surely among the first. Maclennan was winning races in New Jersey and Maryland during the early 1940s and currently, at 73, still trains horses in Florida, New Jersey and Pennsylvania. Two other early pioneer trainers were Ida Mae Parrish, 71, a Massachussets County Fair trainer, and Wilhelmina Trueman, deceased, who trained horses at Delaware Park during the mid-1940s.

According to unofficial records, there are approximately 350 licensed women trainers in America and several have outstanding records, including Sue Sadlacek, who ranks among the top 10 trainers in New York, the toughest racing circuit in the game.

Mary Edens trains the racing stable of Mrs. H.D. Paxson of New Hope, Pa., and is highly respected for her consistent work with grass specialists in Florida and New Jersey. Paxson, the leading owner and breeder in Pennsylvania, owned and bred two Eclipse Award-winning champions during the 1970s.

Jacqueline Branham and Denise Pace also have enjoyed considerable training success in the 1980s. Both have been among the top winning trainers at Tampa Bay Downs the past five years and both have made the top 10 lists at Calder racetrack in Florida and Churchill Downs in Kentucky.

The bottom line is this: No other professional sport is so wide open to women. All the doors are open. If a woman wants to train, ride, care for or be involved with horses, there are no rules, no practices, nothing to inhibit her interest. At most racetracks, at least 40 percent of the backstretch help — including outriders, exercise riders, hot walkers, grooms, veterinarians and other employees — are women. If a woman seeks employment with track management, or wishes to write about or photograph racing, or to engage in policy-making decisions, the sport is ready for her to make her contribution. Dozens of women have done so since 1969, when the sex barrier was shattered by three courageous female jockeys; hundreds more will do so in the years to come.

# Track's dimensions influence the outcome

One of the most important and fascinating aspects of racing is the way the racing surface and the dimensions of the track influence the results.

Like baseball stadiums of different sizes and shapes that may favor pitchers or home-run hitters, each track has its own peculiarities that favor certain running styles or post positions. The track's sensitivity to moisture, its drainage system, the slope of its turns and other physical characteristics make a significant difference in the way races are run.

Belmont Park in New York features a wide, turning course, 1½ miles in circumference; Aqueduct, Hollywood Park, Atlantic City and Saratoga are 1⅛-mile tracks, but each has slightly different contours, widths and stretch lengths. Churchill Downs, home of the Kentucky Derby, is a one-mile track with narrow turns and the third-longest stretch in American racing (1,234.5 feet). Santa Anita Park is a one-mile track with softer turns and a shorter stretch (990 feet).

Some of the differences in track design are quite subtle and others quite severe, but in each case they affect horse performance and jockey strategy.

At Churchill Downs, for instance, the long homestretch may give slow-breaking types an ideal opportunity to fire their best stretch run, but this is not true at all distances. In races of 1-1/16 mile, which begin in front of the grandstand and require a complete trip around the track, the starting gate is positioned so close to the first turn that most races are won and lost in the first quarter mile.

49

Stretch runners and horses forced to break from outside post positions (by the luck of the post position draw) have a lot to overcome in 1 and 1/16-mile races at Churchill Downs. If they do not get off to a fast start, they face the prospect of an extremely wide trip. And when a horse races wide, especially in the first of two or more turns, it expends precious energy while losing ground. Such a predicament might be called bad racing luck, but it does not happen because of haphazard chance.

A daring jockey stuck with a bad post position may try to compensate for this dilemma by rushing his horse out of the starting gate, but the strategy may backfire. If the horse gets caught in an early duel for the lead, if he gets hung out wide in its bid for position, he may tire abruptly before the stretch comes into play.

Knowing these things about 1 and 1/16-mile races at Churchill Downs can be an invaluable aid to watching races there, as well as at all tracks where the starting gate is positioned close to the first turn.

Observing the break from the starting gate will help explain many poor performances. Any time should a horse win or finish strongly despite taking a wide trip around the first turn, he will deserve extra credit.

This principle of interpreting races in the context of the way the track influences the outcome is vital to superior handicapping and will help the casual fan make sense of many strange results. Likewise, the player may find it easier to plot the way a race is going to be run. Remember, the shortest distance between points always is a straight line. At the track, the inside rail is the straightest and shortest line from start to finish.

Canterbury Downs, which will feature a one-mile dirt track and a 7-furlong (⅞ of a mile) infield turf course, is expected to offer main track races for thoroughbreds at 5 furlongs, 5½, 6 and 6½, with the latter distance starting from the chute in the extreme right-hand corner of the backstretch (See illustration). Also, there will be races around two turns at one mile, 1 mile and 70 yards, 1-1/16 miles, 1⅛ miles, 1-3/16 miles and 1¼ miles. The 1¼-mile race will begin out of chute extending out of the homestretch. The turf course will be opened for use in 1986.

Although each racing distance is measured to within ⅛ inch of accuracy, they are never true *racing* distances.

Each distance is marked by a 10-foot-high pole, but in every case, the starting gate is positioned approximately 20 yards *behind* the pole, to give the horses a running start. The race officially begins when the lead horse passes through the electronic beam at the first pole. This beam triggers the electronic timer and while the race is in progress, the lead horse will trigger other beams at other poles, including a beam at the finish line. This permits accurate electric tim-

## Canterbury Downs racetrack

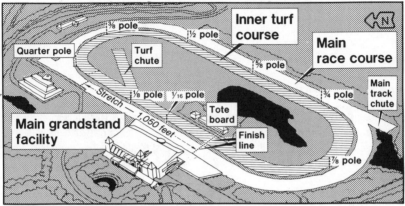

Source/Canterbury Downs   Star and Tribune graphic

ing of the complete race as well as the internal fractions along the way.

The ⅝ pole, also known as the 5-furlong pole, refers to ⅝ of a mile from the finish line.

The quarter pole is 2 furlongs from the finish; the ¾ pole, or 6-furlong pole, is ¾ of a mile from the finish, and the 1/16th pole is 1/16th of a mile from the finish. The finish line is not marked by a furlong pole. For the purposes of assisting track patrons and jockeys, there is a line strung about 20 feet above ground that represents the finish line and a pole is also placed along the inside rail with a bull's-eye target on top of it.

The actual finish is a precisely calibrated line set up exclusively for use by the photo-finish camera.

All the furlong poles and distance markers are used as reference points by racing officials, jockeys, trainers and knowledgeable fans in every English-speaking country where races are run.

# Canterbury's layout will make a difference

Months before a single race is run at Canterbury Downs, we could guess how the configuration of the track may influence some race results.

Consider Churchill Downs. At Churchill, in 1 and 1/16th-mile races, the starting gate is positioned so close to the first turn that many races are won and lost in the first quarter of a mile.

At Canterbury, no such problem is anticipated for 1 and 1/16th-mile races because the starting gate will be set approximately ⅛ mile away from the first turn. This will give each jockey 12 to 13 seconds of running time to avoid extremely wide turns, while minimizing the importance of post positions.

If Canterbury elects to run races at 1 mile, the starting gate would be positioned 1/16th mile closer to the first turn. At that distance, post positions would be as important as they are in Churchill's 1 and 1/16th-mile events.

The same may be true for races contested around one turn at 5 and 5½ furlongs. At 5 furlongs, a distance normally reserved for 2-year-olds in May and June, the starting gate will be positioned on the backstretch barely ⅛ mile before the far turn.

At 5½ furlongs, the run to the first turn will be lengthened 1/16th of a mile, which should reduce the pressure to gain a contending position out of the starting gate. But a thoroughbred in full flight can be expected to reach the turn in 17 seconds. That would be enough time to avoid a wide trip but not to avoid a traffic jam.

Also, from start to finish, a 5½ furlong race takes approximately 65 seconds to complete. This maximizes the impact of what happens in the first 17 seconds, because only 48 seconds of racing remain, including 24 seconds on the turn when it is difficult to improve position. Thus, in sprints of 5½ or even 6 furlongs, a poor start or traffic jam might be the difference between victory and a dismal finish.

These design characteristics are found at racetracks around the country and play a key role in the strategy of short and long races. This is true for Canterbury Downs, Santa Anita, Saratoga or any thoroughbred racetrack. The same principal applies to the way races are run over wet or drying out racing strips.

Most wet-track races are won by fast-breaking horses having the advantage of not getting splashed in the face. Most wet racing strips contribute to this tendency because they tend to become slightly faster before the water seeps into the top soil. (The next time you journey to an ocean beach, run along the water's edge. You will know what it feels like to be on a first-class racing strip immediately after a rainfall. In racing, they call a track like that sloppy, but really it is *wet fast*.)

A few racetracks in America do not get packed down so tightly when rain falls. Some get mushy right away or the water seeps right through the surface. These tracks have unusual drainage systems or other peculiarities. Some are brand new and need time to establish their true consistency and some are tiring tracks that inhibit front-running speedsters even when they are dry.

No one can predict how Canterbury's racing surface will behave in wet or dry conditions until the first season is well under way.

According to Joe King, the track superintendent for the New York Racing Association who served as a consultant on the Canterbury project, the track has been constucted with two layers of crushed limestone for a base, with 4,000 to 5,000 tons of top soil placed on the surface, spread evenly to a depth of 4 inches. The upper layer of the base will be 9 inches and the top soil placed over the base will be a blend of sand, silt and clay packed down to 3¼ or 3½ inches for racing. This top soil, called the track cushion, will provide shock absorption for thoroughbreds in motion. The track will be banked 4½ degrees on the turns.

King believes drainage at Canterbury Downs will be excellent because the water naturally will flow off the track surface toward gutters placed along the infield side of the rail. But even in dry weather, the condition of the track may vary from very fast to slow depending upon other factors in track maintenance.

To keep a track safe and uniform, the superintendent must monitor the moisture content while manicuring the track cushion constantly. When bad weather threatens, the superintendent may order his crew to work through the night to press down on the cushion with heavy rollers to assist drainage. This process, called *sealing the track,* makes the racing strip faster than normal. So does the process known as *scraping the track.*

When a track is scraped or rolled by heavy equipment, it tends to get harder, firmer, faster. Race clockings get faster. Front-runners win more than their share of races.

Approximately two to three times a week, regardless of weather, the track maintenance crew usually has to scrape top soil away from the inside rail because of the natural tendency of the soil to drift there. At most tracks, this brings about a slight **track bias,** a tendency to give an edge to horses racing along the rail. Sometimes this tendency, or an opposite bias, becomes so pronounced that no race can be successfully handicapped without taking it into account.

# There will be many types of races at Canterbury

Races are scheduled at thoroughbred tracks according to the quality of horses stabled on the grounds. At Belmont Park in New York, the horse population includes a large number of stakes horses and royally bred 2-year-olds. At Waterford Park in West Virginia, there are no stakes horses and few capable of competing at Belmont.

Once a year, Waterford Park schedules a $75,000 race that attracts horses from Belmont and other major tracks. But this is a one-way street. Belmont never schedules races to attract Waterford horses.

Canterbury Downs is a new track, a new opportunity for owners and trainers to consider. Yet it is no threat to deplete the Belmont entries. Ditto for Waterford. We are not likely to witness a mass exodus of horses from New York to Minnesota, nor will there be an army of horses shipped from West Virginia to Minneapolis. In fact, there probably will be less than half a dozen Waterford horses here during the entire 1985 season. The horse population stabled at Canterbury figures to be between these extremes.

At Canterbury, there will be 32 stakes races worth a combined total of $1.2 million and purses will total about $6.5 million over the 83 racing dates. While neither sum is earth-shattering, the Canterbury stakes program should succeed in attracting high-quality horses from Ak-Sar-Ben in Omaha, Woodbine in Toronto, Arlington Park in Chicago and some popular New York and California stars. The purpose of a stakes schedule is to lure *name* horses and jockeys for special events while attracting quality stables for the full season.

Intense competition for quality horses has put the squeeze on several eastern tracks while altering the Midwest racing calendar. For instance, Churchill Downs, open from May to October the last two years, has decided to return to its traditional spring and fall schedule in 1985, abandoning its summer season. This is a lucky break for Canterbury, which will compete for Churchill's top racing stables with Arlington Park and Ak-Sar-Ben. This competition, especially for stakes horses, will continue throughout the summer and the outcome will depend upon a mixture of personal diplomacy and economic considerations.

During the winter and spring of 1985, horsemen throughout the country were evaluating Canterbury's facilities, its stakes schedule and its every-day purse structure. At every track, the quality of racing depends upon which stables settle in for the entire meeting and which choose to go elsewhere. But no matter the level of class of the eventual horse population, there always will be different types of races on the daily schedule. We should define some of these basic racing categories before we proceed further with our discussion about class in racing.

**Maiden races/** For nonwinners. Separate races for 2-year-olds; 3-year-olds; 3-year-olds and up; 4-year-olds; 4-year-olds and up; fillies; and fillies and mares. These age and sex groupings also are found in claiming races, allowance races and stakes as defined below.

**Claiming races/** Horses are entered in a given race *for sale* at a specific price. Any registered owner or trainer with money on deposit with the track bookkeeper can submit a claim on any horse entered in a claiming race, providing the claim is submitted no later than 10 minutes before post time. When such a claim is made, no one knows about it until after the race is over, but the horse changes ownership as soon as the starting gate opens. The purse money, if any, goes to the original owner.

Claiming races are scheduled for horses priced at $1,500 minimum at Waterford Park to a maximum of $1 million at Belmont and other top tracks. At Belmont, the minimum claiming price is $12,500, while at Arlington it is $5,000. At Canterbury, the minimum claiming price will be $4,000.

Purses for claiming races are scaled to the price of the horses entered. If a race is scheduled for a field of $5,000 claimers, it may have a $5,000 purse. If scheduled for $10,000 claimers, it may have a $7,500 purse. Using these two purses as a guide, the purse for a $20,000 claiming race would probably be about $10,000.

Claiming prices offer a guide to the overall ability of a given horse or the entire field. Any horse capable of winning a $20,000 claiming race is probably faster than a $10,000 horse. Obviously, the owner of a solid $20,000 horse would be foolish to drop him into a

$10,000 claiming race. Surely another owner or trainer would claim him.

Claiming races provide a convenient means to establish class levels for the majority of racehorses who are not stakes performers. More claiming races are scheduled than any other type of race.

**Stakes/** Open to the best horses on the grounds and other top quality horses around the country. The owner pays nominating and entry fees to confirm a reservation in the race. These fees are added to the money put up by the track, increasing the total purse for the stakes. Weights are assigned according to the horse's winning record or by the judgment of the track's official handicapper. When weights are assigned by the track handicapper, the idea is to equalize the field by giving the best horse the most weight to slow him down relative to the competition. For obvious reasons, these races are called *handicaps*.

**Allowance races/** Open to stakes horses, maidens or claimers, although none are offered for sale in the these races. Entries are restricted according to money or races won. Weights are assigned according to the amount of money won during the recent past or according to lifetime winning records. Purses tend to be higher than most claiming races but lower than stakes. On the average racing program, the feature race often will be an allowance race if it is not a stakes.

# Two dynamic relationships exist at every track

The four basic categories of races — maidens, claiming, allowances and stakes — are subdivided by age, distance, turf course or main track. There are other race categories, some of which will be seen regularly at Canterbury Downs.

**Maiden claiming race/** As the name indicates, this is a claiming race for nonwinners.

**Maiden special weight/** A maiden race for nonclaimers in which all the horses are assigned the same weight. Typically, these are races for the best bred or the most promising nonwinners.

When an owner enters a horse in a $5,000, $10,000 or $30,000 maiden claiming race, the price indicates the relative *class* of the field. Cheap maiden claiming races attract proven losers or horses that have shown only modest promise in limited careers or workouts. Expensive maiden claiming races — $30,000 to $50,000 — may include faster horses, including some who could win a typical maiden special weight race.

At Belmont Park during September, the average winning time for maiden 2-year-olds at 6 furlongs is 1:11-4/5. This average clocking was computed via 100 maiden special weight races at Belmont during the 1980s. September was chosen because 2-year-olds have been exposed to racing by then.

At the same racetrack during the same time-frame, the average winning time for 2-year-old maiden claimers priced at $25,000 was 1:13-4/5, or two full seconds slower than the average maiden special weight race.

At the $50,000 maiden claiming level, the average winning time was 1:12-4/5, while $75,000 maidens averaged 1:12 flat.

These comparisons confirm two dynamic relationships that exist at every racetrack in America.

■ *There is a proportionate relationship between class and time.* Speaking generally, the higher the class level, the faster the clocking.

■ *There is always a point on the claiming class ladder that produces a faster average clocking than nonclaiming races.* This is true for maiden claimers when they are compared with maiden special weight races and it is true for all other claiming races vs. allowance races. (Again, the higher the claiming price, the more likely the time of the race will equal the average clocking for maiden special weight, or allowance races).

## Belmont Park maiden comparison

| Race category | 6 furls. avg. time | Typical purse |
|---|---|---|
| Maiden special weight | 1:11/45 | $19,000 |
| Maiden $50,000 claiming | 1:12-4/5 | 14,000 |
| Maiden $75,000 claiming | 1:12 | 16,000 |

**Allowance races** are open to winners and maidens, with no claiming prices attached, but the conditions of eligibility contain restrictions. These restrictions bar some horses from each contest and are published in a booklet called the *condition book*. The condition book, which is written by the track's racing secretary, contains the eligibility rules for *all* races during a two-week period. Trainers and owners examine the conditions of these races to determine where they want to enter their horses.

The following are some frequently written conditions for allowance races at most tracks:

**For nonwinners of two races/** Open to the winners of zero or one race.

**For nonwinners of a race other than maiden or claiming/** Open to maidens, winners of a maiden special weight, or a maiden claiming race. Also open to winners of one *or more* claiming races, because claiming races do not count against the horse's eligibility for this type allowance race.

**For nonwinners of three races/** Open to winners of zero, one or two races.

**For nonwinners of three races other than maiden or claiming/** Open to winners of zero, one, two, or three nonclaiming races.

At each track, the purse structure for allowance races is scaled according to the degree of difficulty involved. Logically, races that exclude winners of two races are easier to win (and have lower purses) than allowance races that include winners of three races.

When comparing the quality of allowance races between tracks, it is important to appreciate the purse structure at that track. Obviously, allowance races at Waterford Park will not be as tough as the same category of race at Churchill Downs. Nor will the Churchill race be as tough as the one at Belmont.

## Allowance race purse comparison

| Nonwinners of a race other than maiden or claiming | |
|---|---|
| Belmont Park | $21,000 |
| Churchill Downs | 10,000 |
| Waterford Park | 3,300 |
| **Nonwinners of three races other than maiden or claiming** | |
| Belmont Park | $29,000 |
| Churchill Downs | 15,000 |
| Waterford Park | 4,700 |

Purses at Belmont are superior to purses at Churchill and purses at Churchill are vastly superior to those at Waterford. Although the vast majority of Waterford allowance-race winners would be overmatched at both tracks, the best horses from Churchill would compete successfully at Belmont. Every season, a few such *shippers* make the grade at Belmont as they do at other top class tracks. On the other hand, when Belmont horses are shipped to Churchill Downs, they may have a distinct class advantage. This class advantage is sometimes nullified by other factors, including current physical condition or suitability to the distance, but frequently it is the key to victory.

# John Henry is in a class by himself

The subject of class in racing does not begin and end with racing categories, claiming prices or purses.

Class is priceless, indefinite. Class is grace under pressure; it is quality, guts, determination.

A $25,000 claiming price for a 3-year-old gelding does not necessarily mean the horse is worth $25,000. For various reasons, the trainer may be running the horse below or above its true worth.

Perhaps the stable needs cash to pay some bills. Often, the trainer will enter the horse over its competitive level or at the wrong distance to give it a prep race. The trainer might drop the horse into a $17,500 claiming race the next time for a serious try at a purse.

Evaluating trainer intention is another intriguing facet of the racing game and is implicitly related to the subject of class.

Some trainers are extraordinarily gifted in placing their horses at their best competitive levels, while many repeatedly underestimate their best prospects. A case in point is 10-year-old John Henry, the world's leading money winner.

John Henry began his racing career in Louisiana as a 2-year-old. John Henry was trained that year by 26-year-old Phil Marino. Marino liked the gelding and thought well enough to keep him out of claiming races that season, meanwhile winning a small stakes race at Louisiana Downs.

The next year, Marino continued to enter John Henry in modest allowance races, with mediocre results.

Marino was convinced the horse had no future in top company, so he decided to drop John Henry in class, entering him in a $25,000 claiming race at the Fairgrounds racetrack in New Orleans on Feb. 8, 1978. John Henry finished sixth. Two weeks later, the gelding was entered in another $25,000 claiming race, finishing 10th. A month after that, he managed a third-place finish in a similar race.

No claim was filed for John Henry. No trainer or owner at the Fairgrounds was willing to spend $25,000 for him. Trainer Marino did not object, however, when a mutual friend arranged for the horse to be sold to Sam Rubin, a retired New York businessman.

Rubin had no other horses in training and only wanted to have something to root for in his visits to the track. He worked out a deal with trainer Robert Donato, a little-known horseman who specialized in one-horse stables.

Donato looked at John Henry's record and watched him work out. On May 21, 1978, he entered the gelding at Aqueduct for $25,000. John Henry won, but once again nobody claimed him, which was perfectly logical. John Henry had established his *class level* by running modestly in several claiming races, all at the same $25,000 level.

No one close to the horse or reading his record could see he soon would be worth considerably more.

But trainer Donato had been thinking about an experiment. He wondered if John Henry would appreciate a race on grass, something he never had tried. Donato knew the gelding's obscure sire, Ole Bob Bowers, came from a breeding line that produced good grass horses. The trainer decided to see for himself. On June 1, 1978, at Belmont Park, John Henry was entered in a $35,000 claiming race on the turf course. The 3-year-old gelding won the race by 14 lengths and never was entered in a claiming race again.

By the end of 1979, John Henry was an established stakes winner on the turf. How much was he worth? Surely more than $35,000, but considerably less than much slower horses who still had complete genitalia.

John Henry, the gelding, could not be sold for millions of dollars to a breeding syndicate. At the bottom line, he was worth only what he could win on the track.

In 1980, Rubin turned the horse over to V.J. (Lefty) Nickerson for a serious stakes racing campaign. The year after that, the 5-year-old gelding was moved to California, where he has remained since in the care of trainer Ron McAnally.

Through his 2-, 3- and 4-year-old racing seasons, John Henry earned the modest sum of $280,000. He was a good horse, a stakes performer, but no one yet knew his true worth or his true level of class. Who could have known that John Henry would rewrite the record books and still be going strong at age 10.

In 1980, John Henry began to assert himself, winning $925,000.

At age 6, he gave owner Rubin quite a few thrills, winning $1.79 million, including the inaugural running of the Arlington Million in a last-gasp effort over The Bart, owned by Franklin Groves of Minnesota. For his exploits, Rubin's horse was voted 1981 Horse of the Year. Four years and several millions of dollars later, what is John Henry worth?

He is not a sprinter and he is much less effective on dirt tracks than he is on the turf. He is 10 years old and his racing days are numbered.

Surely, there is no price to be set for him. Surely, we can not specify his *class*. But if John Henry does not have a ton of it, then there never was a horse who did.

# The Flamingo Stakes
# of 1984

Occasionally, a single race will illustrate many things about the racing game. Such a race was the Flamingo Stakes of 1984.

Run at Hialeah Park each year, the 1⅛-mile Flamingo is an important stakes on the road to the Kentucky Derby. It helps identify legitimate Triple Crown prospects, while typically advancing their physical condition. The 1984 Flamingo did all of that and more.

The official program page is reprinted with the permission of Hialeah Park. It includes the official saddle cloth number for each horse, along with the owner's name (upper left), trainer's name (upper right), jockey silks (centered above each horse's name) the weight assignment (122 or 118), breeding information, including the year the horse was foaled, plus the sire and dam, (placed under each horse's name). The jockey is listed to the right of the weight along with an early odds estimate, called the morning line.

The overwhelming favorite was Devil's Bag, rated at 1-2 odds in the morning line. Devil's Bag, a son of Halo out of the mare Ballade, was so highly regarded because he had won six straight races very impressively. Many experts were convinced he would become a sure-fire Triple Crown winner. His trainer, Hall of Famer Woody Stephens, 71, repeatedly labeled the colt, "the best horse I've ever trained."

Dr. Carter, owned by Minnesota's Francis A. Genter and named for a Minneapolis surgeon, was billed as a terrific Triple Crown prospect, the second best 3-year-old in the country, the only serious threat to Devil's Bag.

Trainer John Veitch, 35, who developed the good horse Alydar

## FIRST HALF OF LATE DAILY DOUBLE
## EXACTA WAGERING ON THIS RACE

| WIN | PLACE | SHOW |
|-----|-------|------|
|     |       |      |

**1⅛ MILES**

### ELEVENTH RACE
#### "FLAMINGO STAKES"
#### $365,000 Minimum Guaranteed (Grade I)

FOR THREE YEAR OLDS. By subscription of $250 each if made on or before Saturday, December 3, 1983, or $500 each if made on or before Friday, February 3, 1984, or by supplementary nomination of $12,500 each by Thursday, March 1, 1984. $1,500 to pass the entry box, Starters to pay $2,000 additional with $350,000 guaranteed to the First Five Finishers The added money and all fees to be divided 60% to the winner, 20% to second, 11% to third, 6% to fourth and 3% to fifth. Sixth place on down $5,000 each from the $365,000 guaranteed purse. Weights: Colts and Geldings, 122 lbs.; Fillies, 117 lbs. Non-winners of a Sweepstakes allowed, 4 lbs. FLAMINGO CUP to winning owner. Replica to the trainer.
Early Closing Saturday, December 3, 1983 with 97 nominations.
Late closing Friday, February 3, 1984 with 10 nominations. Total 107 nominations.

Track Record—HIS MAJESTY (5) 119 lbs. 1:46⅖; January 17, 1973

### MAKE SELECTION BY NUMBER

| | Owner | | Trainer | Jockey/Morn. Line |
|---|---|---|---|---|
| **1** | J. M. LEVITCH — Black, Red "JL", Red Sleeves, Red Cap — **HIGH ALEXANDER** 122 — Dk.b. or br.c.(1981), Zen—Zar Alexander | OWNER | | 50 — Constantino HERNANDEZ |
| **2** | FRANCES A. GENTER STABLE — Light Blue, Gold Hoops, Gold Cap — **DR. CARTER** (F) 122 — Gr.c.(1981), Caro—Gentle Touch | J. M. VEITCH | | 2 — JORGE VELASQUEZ |
| **3** | O. M. PHIPPS — Black, Cherry Collar, Cuffs and Cap — **Time For A Change** 122 — Ch.c.(1981), Damascus—Resolver | A. PENNA, SR. | | 5 — J. D. BAILEY |
| **4** | ELSIE A. ROSE — Pink, Red Rose, Pink Cap — **REXSON'S HOPE** (F) 122 (S) — Dk.b. or br.c.(1981), Rexson—Abe's Miss | H. J. ROSE | | 30 — ROBERT GAFFGLIONE |
| **5** | RUSTIC WOODS FARMS — Navy Blue, Navy Blue "RWF" on Beige Ball, Beige Band on Sleeves, Navy Blue Cap — **Heir to the Throne** (F) 118 — B.c.(1981), Cormorant—Cheeveetah | P. M. MAXWELL | | 50 — GENE ST. LEON |
| **6** | H. VALDES — Mustard, Royal Blue Collar and Cuffs, Royal Blue Cap — **PAPA KOO** (F) 122 — Gr.c.(1981), Judger—How Dear | D. DAVIS | | 30 — ODIN LONDONO |
| **7** | HICKORY TREE STABLE — Green, Yellow Sash, Yellow Blocks on Sleeves, Green Cap — **DEVIL'S BAG** 122 — B.c.(1981), Halo—Ballade | W. C. STEPHENS | | 1-2 — EDWARD MAPLE |
| **8** | H. ALLEN — White, Red Cross Sashes, Red Blocks on Sleeves, White Cap — **MASTERFUL** (F) 118 (S) — Gr.c.(1981), Jet Diplomacy—Nativeness | E. JACOBS | | 50 — JEAN CRUGUET |

S—Denotes Registered Florida Stallion          F—Denotes Registered Florida Breds

### Selections 7-2-3-4

in 1978, believed Devil's Bag was overrated and openly predicted an upset victory for his colt.

Veitch explained his reasons the day before the race. "When Devil's Bag was a 2-year-old last year (1983), he looked very impressive because he was more mature than the rest of his peers."

Veitch pointed out that Devil's Bag had raced only once beyond a mile and never had to negotiate two turns.

"Beginning with the Flamingo (1⅛ miles), he's going to be meeting stronger horses at longer distances and I'll be quite surprised if he continues to dominate his opposition."

Veitch concluded this interview with a prediction: "I'm very confident Dr. Carter will beat Devil's Bag. But I'm worried to death about the other horse in this race, Time for A Change. He's had the benefit of three races beyond a mile this year and that gives him a tremendous edge so early in the season."

Time For A Change was not as well known as Devil's Bag or Dr. Carter. As a 2-year-old, trainer Angel Penna Sr. started the colt only twice, winning a maiden race by 10 lengths at Saratoga. The colt was 11th in the Hopeful stakes after suffering a minor injury. In November, Penna shipped him to Florida to prepare for the spring classics.

Time For A Change was on a program of long, slow gallops and well-spaced workouts that emphasized finishing ability rather than speed. On Jan. 17 and 31, Penna entered the colt in two allowance races at 1-1/16 miles for experience. When the colt won the second race impressively, Penna knew he was ready for stakes.

"I think he's a good horse, getting better," Penna said at the time. On Feb. 11, Time For A Change won the Everglades Stakes, a $50,000 prep for the Flamingo. The time for the 1⅛-mile distance was 1:47-1/5, the second-fastest in Hialeah history.

But his impressive victory was barely noticed in the shadow cast by the publicity surrounding Devil's Bag. Then came the Flamingo Stakes.

The largest Florida racing crowd in 15 years showed up at Hialeah to see if Devil's Bag could live up to his advance billing. More than 100 newspapers, magazines and television stations were there to cover the new *wonder horse*. They should have paid more heed to John Veitch.

Time For A Change and Devil's Bag dueled for the lead through the first 7 furlongs, each trying to assume control of the race, pressing against their individual limits. But the effort cost Devil's Bag dearly. He couldn't shake loose from Time For A Change. Leaving the final turn, Devil's Bag was losing ground, fading out of contention.

Dr. Carter, under jockey Jorge Velasquez, moved to the outside on the final turn to launch his patented stretch run. Most expected Dr. Carter would rush easily past an exhausted Time For A Change.

But Penna's training regimen was showing through. Time For A Change was at his best, too strong to be denied. Dr. Carter was unable to gain any ground on his rival through the final 70 yards, losing the race to Time For A Change by a head in 1:47 flat.

It was probably the best single performance turned in by a racehorse in 1984, but its effects were not all positive on the horses involved.

Time For A Change took ill and was slow to recover, missing all the major stakes of 1984. Dr. Carter took ill in Kentucky and did not win a race until Jan. 14, 1985. Rexson's Hope, who passed a tired Devil's Bag for third, failed to win a race for the rest of the year and Devil's Bag was only able to win a a pair of minor races in Kentucky before his connections retired him to stud.

Far from being a sensible prep stakes on the road to the Kentucky Derby, the 1984 Flamingo may have stunted the conditioning of every horse in the race.

"It was too tough, too early in the season," explained Billy Turner Jr., the former trainer of Triple Crown champion Seattle Slew. "All the hype about Devil's Bag being a wonder horse made everybody want to try just a little bit harder to be the first to beat him."

Sometimes a hard race helps advance the conditioning process; other times it will knock the horse for a loop.

# Winning trainer Jack Van Berg

In 1984, trainer Jack Van Berg reached the goal of his life. Make that two goals. He won his first Triple Crown race (with Gate Dancer in the Preakness) and was voted an Eclipse Award as the nation's top trainer.

Both accomplishments were long overdue.

Since 1968, Van Berg has won seven national championships, second only to Hirsch Jacobs, the 11-time titleholder between 1933 and 1944. Van Berg, 48, is the winningest trainer in racing history, with more than 4,000 victories to his credit, including a record-shattering 496 in 1976 — 144 more than any other trainer has won in a single season.

"Awards don't mean a lot to me," Van Berg said recently, "but the Eclipse Award is something special.

"I honestly think I should've won it in '76. Not only did we win more races in history, but we broke the record for most money won too."

Van Berg is particularly proud of the $2,976,196 he won that year even though his earnings record didn't last long. "It's been broken five times since," he said. "But purses have skyrocketed these past few years and I didn't have more than a few stakes winners in my barn. We did it all with claiming horses and cheap purses."

Van Berg grew up in Columbus, Neb., in a thoroughbred-racing family. His father, Marion H. Van Berg, was one of the most successful racehorse owners of all time.

"Things are not very different now than they were when my father set things up in the early '50's," Jack Van Berg said. "We've always specialized in the cheaper horse. Dad was the greatest horseman I ever saw and the only thing I've done is follow through with what he showed me."

Marion Van Berg, who died in 1971, was a racetrack legend who revolutionized horse ownership during the 1950s and '60's. He bred and bought hundreds of inexpensive thoroughbreds, racing them in his purple and gold stable silks at several Midwest tracks. Between 1952 and 1970, the Van Berg stable won more than 2,500 races and 14 national championships, both world records. Although other trainers sometimes were involved in the operation, Marion Van Berg supervised every last detail.

Jack Van Berg has refined his father's concepts to an art form, hiring several assistant trainers to supervise 30 to 40 horses apiece at the Fair Grounds in New Orleans, Ak-Sar-Ben in Omaha, Arlington Park in Chicago, Oaklawn Park in Hot Springs, Ark., and tracks on both coasts. Van Berg will have about 20 horses at Canterbury Downs, perhaps under the supervision of his son Tim.

"I spend over $72,000 in air travel each year," Van Berg said. "I've got over 200 horses in training and another 100 on a new farm in Kentucky. At least once every two weeks I get to see them all," he said. "I'm using Santa Anita as my home base this winter, but Tim has a good group at the Fair Grounds. The rest are supervised by some of the best assistant trainers in the business.

"We do have better horses now and we have a lot of outside owners, including Ken Opstein." (Opstein, born in Waseca, Minn., owns Gate Dancer). "But the operation is basically the same as it was when my dad was alive. We still like to work with cheap stock; we still like to solve their leg problems; we still enjoy claiming a horse for $10,000 and seeing him win for 20."

Van Berg says there is no secret formula to winning races. "It's getting up at 5 a.m. or earlier, learning to see each horse as an individual, understanding their peculiar habits and precisely watching their diet and training regimen.

"You can't win races by working a horse when he's slightly off his feed or walking with a minor injury," he said. "You can't get a horse to put out his best when he's over- or underworked. And when you run into a very difficult problem horse — one that doesn't want to do what you know he can — that's when you've got to think things through very carefully."

In thinking things through for 20 years, Van Berg has solved problems for many horses, but none has been more perplexing than Gate Dancer, the Preakness winner who was disqualified from the Kentucky Derby and Breeders' Cup Classic because he lugged in on rivals through the stretch.

"I lost a lot of sleep and a lot of hair over this horse," Van Berg said after the Breeders' Cup. "Can you imagine how much money we would've won if he could only keep a straight course."

In his attempt to keep Gate Dancer at peak form and to curb the horse's roguish tendencies, Van Berg designed special blinkers to limit the horse's vision and added a shadow roll over the colt's muzzle to keep him from jumping over shadows on the track. But the real eye-catching piece of equipment was a purple hood that covered Gate Dancer's face and ears.

"I saw a rig like that in Japan and it seemed to help the horse hold his head a bit lower, so he wouldn't pick up so much wind resistance. Also, it blocked some of the crowd noise, which had been spooking him in a few races. For a while, he ran straight and true, winning the Preakness and the Omaha Gold Cup, but in the Breeders' Cup, he did his number again and was dq'd from second to third. I think he's the best horse in the country and the most interesting horse I've ever trained, but he's still trying to beat me and so far I'm not sure he hasn't."

This year, Van Berg said, "I'm going to try something different. If I have one major goal left over from this experience, it is to bring him back to win the Breeders' Cup."

# It's the percentage of wins, not the number

Today we begin to analyze the role of the trainer in the racing equation. Our first step is to consider a few implications of a large body of statistical data, some of which rarely is taken into account by the average horseplayer.

For instance, in 1984, there were more than 4,000 trainers (out of 12,000 total) who failed to win a single race, 3,000 who failed to win five races and 3,000 more who failed to win 10. That's 10,000 trainers who failed to win 10 races in 1984!

To seek lessons in horsemanship from most of these trainers would be like taking batting instruction from the weakest hitters in baseball. Such trainers rarely win sufficient races to pay the feed bills. Usually, they are victims of their own inexperience or incompetence.

Nevertheless, it would be a mistake to dismiss all such trainers as losers. Some are expert horsemen with very few horses in their care, men and women who win fewer than 10 races only because they operate on a small scale, at one or two tracks a year. Actually, if we examine the techniques of these winning horsemen, winning fewer than five or 10 races is not the reliable statistic that it appears. *The number of wins is not nearly as important as the percentage of wins.*

In 1984, out of the same 10,000 trainers who won fewer than 10 races, there were 5,000 who won fewer than one race in 20 attempts (5 percent), while on the opposite end of the scale there were about 200 who won at least 20 percent of the time. Obviously, the 1-for-20 group (5 percent) is a very weak group of trainers, while the 1-for-5 group (20 percent) includes many legitimate experts. Twenty percent is an excellent winning ratio for a trainer, one to compare favorably with the nation's top horsemen. Interestingly, most of the 200-plus trainers who worked so well with limited stock in 1984 were repeaters from prior seasons. These horsemen tended to race with 20 percent success at their favorite track three or more years in succession. Some choose not to travel to other tracks, others own breeding stock and supervise small racing stables in one location.

Generally, these successful, small-time trainers tend to point their few horses for the local season and rarely waste their best winning opportunities. They are unlikely to train a Kentucky Derby prospect, but from a handicapper's point of view, they provide reliable opportunities for longshots every year.

I am reminded of the case of William Stirling Sr., a trainer with few horses who operated in Florida during the 1970s. Stirling rarely won more than 10 races a year and never made the top 10 list at Hialeah or Gulfstream Park. But for several seasons during the 1970s, Stirling had a habit worth noting: Six times out in eight tries, during a span of seven years, Stirling won a Florida race at 25-1 or better odds. Was it coincidence? Hardly.

"If I can win one race a year at long odds, I pay for my entire winter down here," Stirling once explained.·

Did Stirling cheat, or instruct his jockey not to try hard enough, so that his horses would appear to be outclassed in subsequent races?

The evidence says no. Stirling was a very sharp trainer, a trainer who knew his way to the betting windows, a man who advanced the conditioning of his horses by racing them into shape, racing them where they *could not* win. Invariably, the horse's past performance profile would reveal very little ability. On the winning day, Stirling's meal ticket would pay off at long odds, because most of the bettors did not appreciate the development of a winning strategy.

Most of the betting public would only see in the Racing Form that Stirling's horse had been soundly defeated two or three times in succession by 10 or more lengths. But these defeats were not what they appeared. Each race had not been a fair test of the horse's talents. Either it was scheduled at an unsuitable distance or at a class level beyond the horse's capabilities. Yet the trainer knew that each race had served to help the horse reach top physical condition.

Finally, when Stirling was convinced that his horse was fit enough for a winning try, he would make a few key changes. These changes went unnoticed by the majority of bettors, but they were always the same.

All of Stirling's longshot winners had a race within five days of the winning effort and in each case there was a switch to the turf course or to a distance the horse never before attempted.

Remarkably, Stirling had a pattern, a pattern that consistently produced winners at longshot prices and his success was not done with mirrors, or through drugs, or any other illegal or unethical training procedure. Stirling may not have been the best trainer who ever lived, but he certainly knew how to set up a horse for a longshot score. We should keep that in mind as we look at raw statistics that lump together winners and losers. We should be on the lookout for such skilled professionals at Canterbury Downs. In-depth analysis of the trainer and his methods is one of the best ways to pick winners at the track. Indeed, there are trainers at most tracks who rely on a few key patterns for their success. These include some of the biggest names in the sport.

# Past performance profiles provide valuable insights

Studying trainers and their methods is an excellent way to develop a successful handicapping technique. The best trainers tend to repeat winning strategies; the worst repeat their mistakes.

In the hands of one trainer, a horse with good recent form might have excellent winning prospects; in the care of another, the same horse might be lucky to finish fifth.

To win races consistently, a trainer must be able to spot the strengths and weaknesses in his stock. He must have a solid plan, a workable training regimen. He can't repeatedly waste a fit horse in races beyond its talents. The player is making a mistake if he tries to predict horse performance without taking the role of the trainer into account.

At this point we should introduce *the past performance profile*, published by the Daily Racing Form (see illustration). Not only is it a summation of the horse's racing record, it is a window through which the talents, habits and strategies of the trainer can be studied.

For instance, consider the racing history of **Eillo,** the 1984 Eclipse Award-winning sprinter who died unexpectedly of colic a few weeks after he won the $1 million Breeders' Cup Sprint at Hollywood Park on Nov. 10.

The accompanying past performance profile (p.p.'s) is the one that appeared for Eillo in the Breeders' Cup edition of the Daily Racing Form.

(The Daily Racing Form is the most comprehensive racing publication in the world, offering p.p.'s, result charts and statistical data for every track in North America.)

## Eillo

**Own.—Crown Stable**

**126**

Ch. c. 4, by Mr Prospector—Barbs Dancer, by Northern Dancer
Br.—Cohen O A (Fla)
Tr.—Lepman Budd

| | | | | | |
|---|---|---|---|---|---|
| | 1984 | 9 | 7 | 0 | 0 | $159,470 |
| | 1983 | 7 | 4 | 0 | 1 | $48,200 |
| Lifetime 10 11 0 1 $207,670 | Turf | 1 | 0 | 0 | 0 | $200 |

| 6Oct84-8Med | 6f :22² :45 1:09⁴ft | *1-2 124 | 11 12½ 14 15 | PerrtC³ Chief Penk H 93-18 Eillo, Introspective, Rollin on Over 6 |
|---|---|---|---|---|
| 11Sep84-8Key | 6f :22 :44³ 1:08⁴ft | *1-5 120 | 11½ 12 13 19 | Perret C¹ Aw16000 97-19 Eillo, Obgyn, Good Ole Master 6 |
| 21Jly84-5Mth | 6f :22¹ :44⁴ 1:09³sy | *2-5 122 | 11½ 11½ 13 11½ | Perret C⁵ Aw17000 92-16 Eillo, Lordly Love, Her Pal 6 |
| 19Apr84-9OP | 6f :21² :44¹ 1:09 ft | *1 126 | 1hd 1hd 21½ 79 | Perret C⁸ Count Fleet 91-12 Dv'sFrind,AllSoldOut,LuckySlvtion 8 |
| 31Mar84-9GP | 1 ①:46²1:10 1:35 fm*4-5 115 | 1hd 21½10221131 | Perret C³ Aw20000 64-09 HpesMill,BluEmmnull,OutOfHock 11 |
| 5Mar84-9Hia | 7f :23¹ :45³ 1:21⁴ft | *1-3 125 | 1hd 11 13 16 | PrrtC⁵ Sprnt Chmp H 94-23 Eillo, Awesome Count, Victorious 5 |
| 10Feb84-9Hia | 7f :23 :45² 1:21¹ft | *1-3 122 | 1½ 1½ 12½ 13 | Perret C⁴ Aw20000 97-22 Eillo, Brother Liam, Bill Wheeler 6 |
| 28Jan84-8Hia | 6f :22¹ :45¹ 1:08⁴ft | *1-2 122 | 1¹ 1² 12½ 17 | Perret C⁵ Kendall 99-15 Eillo, Compo's Tempo, FastReason 6 |
| 9Jan84-9Hia | 6f :22 :44² 1:08¹ft | 2 115 | 1½ 12½ 12½ 13 | PerretC³ Tallahasee H 102-15 Eillo, Center Cut, In The Bucks 10 |
| 30Nov83-9Crc | 6½f:22¹ :45¹ 1:17³sy | *4-5 119 | 1½ 1½ 2½ 46½ | Perret C¹ Aw17000 90-19 ChnLnk'sDrm,MyMc,CourtosMjsty 6 |

● Nov 6 Hol 4f ft :45 hg     ● Oct 30 SA 6f ft 1:11¹ h     Oct 23 SA 5f ft 1:01 h     Oct 17 SA 4f ft :48 b

Eillo entered the Breeders' Cup Sprint as the favorite. He had won seven of nine starts in 1984, for a total of **$159,470** (upper right corner of the p.p.'s) He had won four straight races between **January 9, 1984** and **March 5, 1984,** all at **Hia**leah Park (date of races and location of track in left hand column of p.p.'s). He had won his last three starts, at three different tracks, (**Mon**mouth Park, **Key**stone, and the **Mead**owlands all in fast clockings **(1:09-3/5, 1:08-4/5, 1:09-4/5)** without ever being headed by another horse.

His two losses, March 31 at **Gulfstream P**ark in Florida and April 19 at **Oaklawn P**ark in Arkansas, came between his two winning streaks and might well have been the fault of the trainer more than the horse.

**Buddy Lepman**, whose name appears in bold type near the weight assignment **(126)** for today's race, is a New Jersey-based trainer who ships to Florida for the winter. For the better part of 28 years, he has been a 15 to 20 percent winner but has had few stakes horses.

Eillo probably was the fastest horse Lepman ever trained. When the colt won those races in Florida, his trainer decided to test him over a longer distance. Horses that can win at a mile or more are much more valuable than horses that have distance limitations.

So Lepman entered Eillo in a turf mile against a very rugged field and watched helplessly as the horse tired badly to finish **11**th, by **31** lengths (The entire running line for each race is a staple part of the p.p.'s. It includes the horse's position after ¼ of a mile, at ½ mile, in mid-stretch and at the finish). Eillo's running line for his March 31 turf race shows that he was **first** by a **head** at the quarter, **second** by 1½ lengths at the half, **10th** by **22** lengths in mid-stretch, and **11th** by **31** at the finish. Jockey Craig **Perret** was aboard Eillo, who broke from post position No. **three**.

Obviously, Eillo didn't care for Lepman's experiment and it may have been the reason the colt failed to hold his speed in the **Count Fleet Stakes** at Oaklawn Park on April 19.

Eillo was a one-dimensional speedball, a colt that wanted to run as hard as he could for as long as he could. Trying him in a tough grass race beyond his normal distance may have confused him. Sometimes it is a good idea not to tamper with a winning formula, a lesson Lepman readily admitted in July at Monmouth Park: "This horse's game is sprint racing and from here on out, if I can bring him back to top form, that's exactly what he's going to do."

Lepman raced Eillo in two allowance races — one at Monmouth on July 21 and one at Keystone racetrack in Pennsylvania on Sept. 11 — before putting him in a minor stakes race at the Meadowlands on Oct. 6. His objective was the $1 million Breeders' Cup Sprint, the biggest purse ever offered to a field of sprinters.

Lepman took Eillo west for a month of workouts to prepare for the big race. The four most recent workouts appear at the bottom of the past performance profile.) On **Oct. 17,** Eillo worked **4** furlongs in **48** seconds breezing at Santa Anita. Oct. 23, the colt worked 5 furlongs in 1:01 handily. Oct. 30, Eillo went 6 furlongs in 1:11-1/5 handily. Four days before the Breeders' Cup Sprint, he went 4 furlongs in 45 seconds handily from the starting gate at Hollywood Park (Handily means without serious urging or whipping; breezing means without any urging at all).

The 6-furlong work and the latest 4-furlong work from the starting gate were both very fast by usual standards (12 seconds per furlong is generally regarded as a good workout). "He's trained very well for this race," Lepman said the morning of the Breeders' Cup. "I think we've recovered his best form just in time."

Eillo won the $600,000 first prize by half a length over fast-closing Commemorate, trained by Laz Barrera. It wasn't the best race Eillo ever ran, but it was the most important. A good trainer had made up for an early-season mistake, but it took him seven months to do it.

# Results charts are racing's version of box scores

Daily Racing Form past performance profiles are derived from Daily Racing Form *result charts.*

These charts — *see illustration next page* — are racing's version of baseball box scores. They spell out the distance and eligibility conditions. They reveal who won, who lost and how each race was run. They include a comprehensive description of what took place, beginning with the name of each horse, the date of its most recent race, age, assigned weight and post position, followed by running positions at key checkpoints from start to finish.

The jockey's name appears immediately to the right of the finishing position, followed by the claiming price if that is the type of race involved. Post-time odds, calculated to $1, appear in the extreme right hand column. Mutuel payoffs appear below the fractional time splits. (Note: Louisiana racetracks use a minimum $3 bet for win, place, show and exactas; California uses $2 for win, place and show and $5 for its exacta bets. Most other tracks use $2 units to calculate all payoffs. Canterbury Downs intends to use $2 for win, place and show but has not yet decided whether it will use a minimum $2 or $3 exacta bet.)

Every result chart includes a detailed report on how that race was run. This report, called the *trackman's comments,* is of considerable value to handicappers. It usually reveals how the pattern of the race took shape, or if any horse encountered traffic trouble. For instance, in the ninth race at the Fair Grounds on Jan. 13, the trackman reports **Chance A Lot,** *was bumped about while between rivals early and was never a threat.* This suggests Chance A Lot may have

**EIGHTH RACE** **6 FURLONGS. (1.09) CLAIMING. Purse $6,000. Fillies. 3-year-olds, non-winners of two races. Weight, 119 lbs. Maidens allowed 7 lbs. Claiming price $25,000. (Winners preferred.)**

## Fair Grounds

**JANUARY 13, 1985**

**Value of race $6,000; value to winner $3,600; second $1,200; third $660; fourth $360; fifth $180. Mutuel pool $61,819. Exacta Pool $99,811.**

| Last Raced | Horse | Eqt. | A. | Wt | PP | St | ¼ | ½ | Str | Fin | Jockey | Cl'g Pr | Odds $1 |
|---|---|---|---|---|---|---|---|---|---|---|---|---|---|
| 30Dec84 $^{7}$FG$^{2}$ | Mac's Prospect | | 3 | 119 | 3 | 6 | $4^{2}$ | $2^{1\frac{1}{2}}$ | $1^{\frac{1}{2}}$ | $1^{2\frac{1}{2}}$ | Romero R P | 25000 | 1.60 |
| 30Dec84 $^{7}$FG$^{3}$ | Joyces Pet | | 3 | 111 | 2 | 4 | $3^{hd}$ | $3^{1}$ | $2^{1\frac{1}{2}}$ | $2^{1\frac{1}{2}}$ | Melancon G$^{5}$ | 25000 | 3.00 |
| 30Dec84 $^{7}$FG$^{4}$ | Dancing Carlene | b | 3 | 114 | 6 | 2 | $6^{hd}$ | $6^{hd}$ | $4^{2}$ | $3^{1\frac{1}{2}}$ | Bass S$^{5}$ | 25000 | 31.20 |
| 6Jan85 $^{4}$FG$^{4}$ | Flaming Goal | | 3 | 116 | 7 | 3 | $10^{1}$ | $9^{2}$ | $6^{1\frac{1}{2}}$ | $4^{nk}$ | Barron V L | 25000 | 29.70 |
| 6Jan85 $^{4}$FG$^{2}$ | Tara B. True | | 3 | 116 | 5 | 1 | $1^{2\frac{1}{2}}$ | $1^{1\frac{1}{2}}$ | $3^{2}$ | $5^{no}$ | Fox W I Jr | 25000 | 6.80 |
| 13Dec84 $^{5}$FG$^{2}$ | Bayside Debut | | 3 | 116 | 4 | 9 | $9^{hd}$ | $8^{1\frac{1}{2}}$ | $5^{2}$ | $6^{3\frac{1}{2}}$ | Copling D | 25000 | 20.10 |
| 31Dec84 $^{8}$FG$^{8}$ | Mrs. Jake | b | 3 | 116 | 12 | 12 | 12 | $11^{3}$ | $8^{3}$ | $7^{2}$ | White J R | 25000 | 49.70 |
| 13Dec84 $^{5}$FG$^{8}$ | Playful Cowgirl | b | 3 | 116 | 10 | 11 | $8^{1}$ | $7^{3}$ | $7^{1}$ | $8^{4}$ | Guidry R D | 25000 | 108.60 |
| 2Jan85 $^{2}$FG$^{1}$ | Fetch the Water | | 3 | 116 | 8 | 7 | $5^{1}$ | $5^{hd}$ | $10^{10}$ | $9^{hd}$ | Melancon L | 25000 | 5.00 |
| 27Dec84 $^{2}$FG$^{1}$ | Decrodare | b | 3 | 119 | 1 | 5 | $2^{hd}$ | $4^{2}$ | $9^{\frac{1}{2}}$ | $10^{11}$ | Ardoin R | 25000 | 24.30 |
| 30Dec84 $^{2}$FG$^{1}$ | Leslie's Goldsand | | 3 | 119 | 11 | 10 | $11^{2}$ | 12 | $11^{hd}$ | $11^{1}$ | Woods C R Jr | 25000 | 9.60 |
| 22Dec84 $^{7}$FG$^{5}$ | Jennifer's Love | b | 3 | 116 | 9 | 8 | $7^{2}$ | $10^{\frac{1}{2}}$ | 12 | 12 | Menard N | 25000 | 49.70 |

**OFF AT 4:22. Start good. Won handily. Time, :22⅕, :46⅘, :59⅗, 1:12⅘ Track fast.**

| $3 Mutuel Prices: | | | | |
|---|---|---|---|---|
| | 3–MAC'S PROSPECT | 7.80 | 5.10 | 4.50 |
| | 2–JOYCES PET | | 5.70 | 4.50 |
| | 6–DANCING CARLENE | | | 9.90 |

**$3 EXACTA (3–2) PAID $20.40.**

**B. f, by New Prospect—Renella McCoy, by Don McCoy. Trainer McDonald Anita J. Bred by Foley Dravo (Ky).**

MAC'S PROSPECT never far back while out from the rail, gained the lead in early stretch, drew clear, and was in hand at the end. JOYCES PET well placed early, came out from the rail to loom a threat, but could not gain on the winner. DANCING CARLENE outsprinted early, rallied to improve her position but did not menace. FLAMING GOAL found her best stride late. TARA B TRUE had speed until early stretch then weakened. FETCH THE WATER raced outside and did not menace.

**Owners—** 1, McMahan R; 2, Gouge G; 3, Scott H; 4, Diaz L; 5, Selig M; 6, Cuevas & Dantin; 7, Leger J E; 8, Despaux Debra; 9, Stevens Farm; 10, Moore D; 11, Saker J E; 12, Voss & Bourque.

**Trainers—** 1, McDonald Anita J; 2, Sebastien James A; 3, Scott Hal; 4, Diaz Lorenzo; 5, Fox William I; 6, Cuevas Delbert; 7, Leger Jake E; 8, Delahoussaye Harold; 9, Walker Charles W; 10, Mustin Harold S; 11, Murphy Paul A; 12, Bourque Anatole.

**Scratched—**Popsalot ( 5Jan85 $^{8}$FG$^{6}$); Van Buren Lass (27Dec84 $^{5}$FG$^{9}$); Vencedor's Queen (30Sep84 $^{7}$LaD$^{10}$); Queen Do Re Mi (22Dec84 $^{7}$FG$^{3}$); A Toast to Paige ( 4Jan85$^{11}$FG$^{3}$).

---

**NINTH RACE** **6 FURLONGS. (1.09) CLAIMING. Purse $8,200. 4-year-olds and upward. Weight, 4-year-olds, 120 lbs.; older, 121 lbs. Non-winners of two races since November 13 allowed 3 lbs.; a race since then, 5 lbs. Claiming price $20,000; if for $18,000 allowed 2 lbs. (Claiming races for $16,000 or less not considered.) (Winners preferred.) (Originally carded for about 7 1/2 furlongs on turf).**

## Fair Grounds

**JANUARY 13, 1985**

**Value of race $8,200; value to winner $4,920; second $1,640; third $902; fourth $492; fifth $246. Mutuel pool $66,680. Exacta pool, $92,493.**

| Last Raced | Horse | Eqt. | A. | Wt | PP | St | ¼ | ½ | Str | Fin | Jockey | Cl'g Pr | Odds $1 |
|---|---|---|---|---|---|---|---|---|---|---|---|---|---|
| 23Dec84 $^{7}$FG$^{2}$ | Flaming Arrow | | 6 | 111 | 8 | 11 | $7^{hd}$ | $7^{\frac{1}{2}}$ | $3^{1\frac{1}{2}}$ | $1^{\frac{1}{2}}$ | Melancon G$^{5}$ | 20000 | 3.40 |
| 6Jan85 $^{7}$FG$^{3}$ | Flakesaway | | 9 | 116 | 12 | 7 | $5^{1}$ | $3^{1}$ | $1^{hd}$ | $2^{2}$ | Fletcher R | 18000 | 6.40 |
| 27Dec84 $^{8}$FG$^{1}$ | Iron Hawk | b | 5 | 118 | 10 | 2 | $4^{hd}$ | $2^{hd}$ | $2^{2\frac{1}{2}}$ | $3^{2\frac{1}{2}}$ | Ardoin R | 18000 | 1.40 |
| 31Dec84 $^{7}$FG$^{7}$ | Confident Son | | 4 | 114 | 5 | 6 | $11^{3}$ | $9^{hd}$ | $6^{3}$ | $4^{1}$ | Poyadou B E | 20000 | 135.00 |
| 23Dec84 $^{7}$FG$^{6}$ | Peace Leader | b | 8 | 114 | 7 | 3 | $3^{1\frac{1}{2}}$ | $4^{1\frac{1}{2}}$ | $5^{1}$ | $5^{\frac{1}{2}}$ | Montoya D | 18000 | 19.90 |
| 23Dec84 $^{7}$FG$^{4}$ | Tin Pan Eustace | b | 5 | 114 | 3 | 4 | $1^{\frac{1}{2}}$ | $1^{1}$ | $4^{2}$ | $6^{2\frac{1}{2}}$ | Faul J H | 20000 | 54.70 |
| 2Jan85 $^{10}$FG$^{4}$ | Wintersole | | 4 | 115 | 1 | 5 | $6^{2\frac{1}{2}}$ | $6^{hd}$ | $7^{1\frac{1}{2}}$ | $7^{1}$ | Woods C R Jr | 20000 | 17.60 |
| 6Jan85 $^{7}$FG$^{4}$ | Say Assagai | | 6 | 115 | 4 | 9 | $9^{\frac{1}{2}}$ | $10^{3}$ | $8^{3}$ | $8^{2}$ | Menard N | 20000 | 29.90 |
| 22Dec84 $^{11}$FG$^{7}$ | Chance A Lot | | 5 | 111 | 2 | 12 | $10^{hd}$ | $11^{2}$ | $9^{2}$ | $9^{2\frac{1}{2}}$ | Murray J H$^{5}$ | 20000 | 4.70 |
| 23Dec84 $^{7}$FG$^{9}$ | Yayo Andariego | | 5 | 114 | 6 | 10 | 12 | 12 | $11^{1}$ | $10^{1}$ | Rubbicco P | 18000 | 55.90 |
| 28Dec84 $^{9}$FG$^{1}$ | Bold n' Exclusive | b | 4 | 112 | 11 | 8 | $8^{hd}$ | $8^{2}$ | $10^{hd}$ | $11^{1}$ | White J R | 20000 | 1.90 |
| 15Dec84 $^{8}$FG$^{7}$ | Flagellate | | 6 | 116 | 9 | 1 | $2^{hd}$ | $5^{1}$ | 12 | 12 | Walker B J Jr | 20000 | 14.40 |

**OFF AT 4:50. Start good. Won driving. Time, :22⅖, :46⅕, :58⅖, 1:11 Track fast.**

| $3 Mutuel Prices: | | | | |
|---|---|---|---|---|
| | 8–FLAMING ARROW | 13.20 | 6.60 | 4.20 |
| | 12–FLAKESAWAY | | 10.80 | 6.30 |
| | 10–IRON HAWK | | | 3.90 |

**$3 EXACTA (8–12) PAID $56.70.**

**Ch. g, by Burning On—To Arms, by Malay Melee. Trainer Zouck Judith H. Bred by Scott D W II (Ky).**

FLAMING ARROW lacked early speed, closed in the middle of the track to gain the lead in deep stretch, and prevailed. FLAKESAWAY never far back gained a slight lead in midstretch, but could not contain the winner. IRON HAWK loomed a threat in midstretch, but could not sustain his effort. CONFIDENT SON found his best stride late. CHANCE A LOT was bumped about while between rivals early and was never a threat.

**Owners—** 1, Scott D W II; 2, Dorignac J P Jr; 3, Tempo Stable; 4, Gabriel H J; 5, Cedar Stable; 6, Hebert S G; 7, Young Gil; 8, Hammack R T; 9, Shaw K & K; 10, Lamb W; 11, Aguillard & Leger; 12, Booge A.

**Trainers—** 1, Zouck Judith H; 2, Dorignac J P III; 3, Walker Charles W; 4, Leggio Andrew Jr; 5, Fishman Donald E; 6, Taylor John L; 7, Trahan Oran; 8, Hammack Revis T; 9, Woods Marshall; 10, Tassistro Sal; 11, Leger Jake E; 12, Deakins William.

**Corrected weight:** Chance A Lot 111 pounds. **Overweight:** Confident Son 2 pounds; Tin Pan Eustace 1.

**Iron Hawk was claimed by Horner Candace; trainer, Horner George.**

**Scratched—**Sing One Song (15Dec84 $^{8}$FG$^{5}$); Train To Glory ( 4Jan85 $^{9}$FG$^{9}$); Lanyons Gray (28Dec84 $^{5}$FG$^{3}$); Judge Lindsey ( 2Jan85 $^{7}$FG$^{6}$); Blushing Lad ( 6Jan85 $^{7}$FG$^{6}$); Flygo (23Dec84 $^{8}$FG$^{8}$).

had an excuse for his dismal ninth-place finish as the $4.70-$1 third choice in the betting.

In the eighth race that same day, the trackman did not notice any such traffic trouble, but he did take note of the way the winner got the job done. *Mac's Prospect, never far back while out from the rail, gained the lead in early stretch, drew clear and was in hand at the end.*

All result charts also include participating owners and trainers, weight corrections and overweights. Corrections occur when incorrect weights were published in the Daily Racing Form or erroneously claimed by the trainer at the time of entry. Overweights occur when jockeys report in heavier than the listed assignment.

Most jockeys are unable to make weight assignments under 115 pounds, but there are exceptions. Willie Shoemaker has consistently weighed under 112 pounds throughout his 36-year career. Because of the desire not to burden race horses with heavy weight assignments, the Jockey Club Scale of weights imposes clear-cut restrictions on thoroughbred jockeys. Any jockey who can not hold his or her weight at or below 118 pounds is not going to get many mounts.

All result charts include the names of horses who were scratched. Scratch time is usually 8 a.m. on race day. But horses may be scratched by the track veterinarian for lameness or for no reason at all with permission of the state stewards. Trainers are sometimes given a free hand to scratch horses without formal approval, but abuse of the privilege is not usually tolerated.

In the post parade, the track veterinarian takes a final look and may order any horse scratched for its own protection. Injuries and deaths sometimes occur, both to jockeys and horses, because no one can foresee all the possibilities. But a strict, expert track veterinarian is fundamental to a program of accident prevention.

Note that the ninth-race chart mentions that *Iron Hawk* was claimed for $18,000. Iron Hawk is a familiar friend of mine. In 1982 and '83, he was running at Tampa Bay Downs for owner George Steinbrenner III, who also owns the New York Yankees. Although the horse had his share of nagging injuries, he was a gritty performer with several victories to his credit.

Five changes of ownership and two years later, trainer George Horner is putting up $18,000 for the horse. Perhaps Horner is thinking that Iron Hawk will be worth more than $18,000 in the near future or maybe he remembers that the colt was very competitive in $30,000 turf races at Calder racetrack in 1982-83. Indeed, Iron Hawk may be a much better horse on grass than on dirt. Furthermore, he appears to be in good physical condition.

Note Iron Hawk's victory in the eighth race at the Fair Grounds on Dec. 27. This information is displayed in the left-hand column of the chart, next to Iron Hawk's name. The chart also reveals that Iron Hawk ran a very good race, finishing a credible third, 2½ lengths behind a swift winner, clocked in 1:11 flat. Compare this clocking with the eighth race (1:12-4/5). Note that Iron Hawk's group ran considerably faster. Had we reproduced the 10th race result chart from the same racing day, we would have seen further proof that Iron Hawk's race was much stronger than the typical $18,000-$20,000 claimer. The 10th race on Jan. 13 was a minor stakes clocked in 1:11 falt, the same clocking recorded by Iron Hawk's $20,000 claimers.

All this intelligence suggested that Iron Hawk might have been worth more than Horner's $18,000 investment, especially if he knew about the colt's hidden turf talents. But we should never be hasty in crediting any trainer with excellent judgement with his claims. Practical results are what count.

During the 30 days following the claim, Horner would have had to raise the colt a required 25 percent in claiming price before being allowed to enter him in a race. This 30-day *jail* period applies to all claimed horses in every racing state and very few trainers are sharp enough to win races at a higher level of competition.

Maybe Horner intended to keep Iron Hawk at the $18,000 level. Maybe he wanted to wait out the jail period for a shot at a race on the grass sometime in the future. Or maybe Horner would never get the best out of Iron Hawk, or perhaps he would enter him in the wrong races only to see the colt's form deteriorate under his care. In either case, we would learn a lot about this particular trainer's skill by charting what he did with after spending $18,000 for one useful horse. From such observations come a winning season.

# Hints about p.p.'s
# and result charts

The accompanying illustration should be of assistance in reading Daily Racing Form past performance profiles (p.p.s). These p.p.s contain an amazing amount of information. Here is how the Daily Racing Form produces them.

Two days before each race day, trainers file entries for all races on the program with the racing secretary. Trainers are responsible for correct weight assignments, including the 5-, 7-, or 10-pound weight concessions given to apprentice jockeys. The track stewards must certify all first-time starters for gate-breaking behavior and the state veterinarian must approve any intended medication.

The Daily Racing Form's trackman transmits the entry data to the regional office in Chicago, where past performances and result charts are stored in computerized files.

On race day, the trackman will record scratches, late weight and jockey changes as he begins to construct his result charts, from which all past performances are derived. During the post parade for each race, which lasts about 11 minutes, the trackman must memorize jockey colors and horses' names, in the same manner as the official track announcer. The trackman's No. 1 job is to provide an accurate race call, which includes the position of every horse in the race at specially designated *points of call*.

The earliest points of call include the break from the gate (called the start) and the positions after one-fourth or one-half or three-fourths of a mile, depending on the distance of the race.

The final three points of call are always the same, except for races beyond two miles, which are rarely scheduled. In all other

# How to read Daily Form past performance profiles

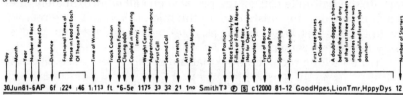

| | Mud | Today's | | | | | | | Today's | | | |
|---|---|---|---|---|---|---|---|---|---|---|---|---|
| Horse | Mark | Weight Color Sex Age Pedigree | | | | | | | Claiming Price | | Earnings Record | |

**Good Hopes** ✶
Own.—Good Hope Farm    **117⁵**

Ch. f.   4   by Ridan—Miss Hopes, by Jet Pilot
Br. Jones H G (Cal)
Tr. Jones H G
Lifetime    20   3   3   4    $23,600

$12,000

| | | | | |
|---|---|---|---|---|
| 1984 | 12 | 3 | 2 | 1 | $20,280 |
| 1983 | 4 | M | 0 | 2 | $1,100 |
| Turf | 4 | 1 | 0 | 1 | $6,500 |

30Jun84–6Hol 6f :22⁴ :46 1:11³ ft *6-5e 117⁵ 3³ 3² 2¹ 1ⁿᵒ SmithT³ ⓕ ⓢ c12000 81-12 GoodHpes,LionTmr,HppyDys 12

Jly 28 Dmr 3f ft :37b    ●Jun 25 Hol 4f ft :46h    ●Jun 20 Hol 3f ft :36²h    May 25 Hol 4f ft :49b

NOTE: Latest workouts are printed under each horse's past performances when they are available. The "bullet" ● indicates it was the best workout of the day at the track and distance.

---

30Jun81–6AP 6f :22⁴ :46 1:11³ ft *6-5e 117⁵ 3³ 3² 2¹ 1ⁿᵒ SmithT³ ⓕ ⓢ c12000 81-12 GoodHpes,LionTmr,HppyDys 12

30Jun81–6AP 6f :22⁴ :46 1:11³ ft *6-5e 117⁵ 3³ 3² 2¹ 1ⁿᵒ SmithT³ ⓕ ⓢ c12000 81-12 GoodHpes,LionTmr,HppyDys 12
**DATE RACE WAS RUN** The day, month and year. This race was on June 30, 1981.

30Jun81–6AP 6f :22⁴ :46 1:11³ ft *6-5e 117⁵ 3³ 3² 2¹ 1ⁿᵒ SmithT³ ⓕ ⓢ c12000 81-12 GoodHpes,LionTmr,HppyDys 12
**NUMBER OF RACE AND TRACK RACED ON** This was the sixth race at Arlington Park (AP.) See the Past Performance section of Daily Racing Form for a complete list of track abbreviations. The ◆ symbol before track indicates it is located in foreign country.

30Jun81–6AP 6f :22⁴ :46 1:11³ ft *6-5e 117⁵ 3³ 3² 2¹ 1ⁿᵒ SmithT³ ⓕ ⓢ c12000 81-12 GoodHpes,LionTmr,HppyDys 12
**DISTANCE OF RACE** The race was at 6 furlongs or ¾ of a mile (there are 8 furlongs in a mile). An "a" before the distance (a6f) denotes an "about" or inexact distance (about 6 furlongs). A circled ⓣ following the distance denotes the race was run on the main turf course; a squared ⓣ a race run on track's inner turf course; ⊡ indicates race run on the inner dirt strip.

30Jun81–6AP 6f :22⁴ :46 1:11³ ft *6-5e 117⁵ 3³ 3² 2¹ 1ⁿᵒ SmithT³ ⓕ ⓢ c12000 81-12 GoodHpes,LionTmr,HppyDys 12
**FRACTIONAL TIMES** The first fraction (.22⅘) is the time of the horse in front after a quarter-mile; the second fraction (.46) is the time of the horse in front at the half-mile point.

30Jun81–6AP 6f :22⁴ :46 1:11³ ft *6-5e 117⁵ 3³ 3² 2¹ 1ⁿᵒ SmithT³ ⓕ ⓢ c12000 81-12 GoodHpes,LionTmr,HppyDys 12
**FINAL TIME OF FIRST HORSE TO FINISH** This is the winner's final time (6 furlongs run in 1:11¾). In all cases, this is the time of the first horse to finish (when the winner is disqualified, this is HIS time, not the time of the horse awarded first money.)

30Jun81–6AP 6f :22⁴ :46 1:11³ ft *6-5e 117⁵ 3³ 3² 2¹ 1ⁿᵒ SmithT³ ⓕ ⓢ c12000 81-12 GoodHpes,LionTmr,HppyDys 12
**TRACK CONDITION** The track was fast (ft).

30Jun81–6AP 6f :22⁴ :46 1:11³ ft *6-5e 117⁵ 3³ 3² 2¹ 1ⁿᵒ SmithT³ ⓕ ⓢ c12000 81-12 GoodHpes,LionTmr,HppyDys 12
**APPROXIMATE CLOSING ODDS** The horse was approximately 6-5 in the wagering. An asterisk (*) preceding the odds indicates the horse was the favorite; an "e" following the odds that it was part of an entry (two or more horses coupled in the wagering); an "f" that horse was in the mutuel field.

30Jun81–6AP 6f :22⁴ :46 1:11³ ft *6-5e 117⁵ 3³ 3² 2¹ 1ⁿᵒ SmithT³ ⓕ ⓢ c12000 81-12 GoodHpes,LionTmr,HppyDys 12
**WEIGHT CARRIED IN THIS RACE** The horse carried 117 pounds. The superior (small) figure indicates that, in this instance, a 5-pound apprentice allowance was claimed. When an apprentice allowance is claimed, the exact amount of the claim is listed.

30Jun81–6AP 6f :22⁴ :46 1:11³ ft *6-5e 117⁵ 3³ 3² 2¹ 1ⁿᵒ SmithT³ ⓕ ⓢ c12000 81-12 GoodHpes,LionTmr,HppyDys 12
**FIRST CALL** The horse was running third, three lengths behind the leader at this stage of the race (at the ¼ mile in this instance). The larger figure indicates the horse's running position, the superior figure his total margin behind the leader. If he had been in front at this point (1³), the superior figure would indicated the margin by which he had been leading the second horse.

30Jun81–6AP 6f :22⁴ :46 1:11³ ft *6-5e 117⁵ 3³ 3² 2¹ 1ⁿᵒ SmithT³ ⓕ ⓢ c12000 81-12 GoodHpes,LionTmr,HppyDys 12
**SECOND CALL** The horse was third at this stage of the race (at the ½ mile in this instance), two lengths behind the leader.

30Jun81–6AP 6f :22⁴ :46 1:11³ ft *6-5e 117⁵ 3³ 3² 2¹ 1ⁿᵒ SmithT³ ⓕ ⓢ c12000 81-12 GoodHpes,LionTmr,HppyDys 12
**STRETCH CALL** The horse was second at this stage of the race, a length behind the leader. The stretch call is made about ⅛ mile from the finish.

30Jun81–6AP 6f :22⁴ :46 1:11³ ft *6-5e 117⁵ 3³ 3² 2¹ 1ⁿᵒ SmithT³ ⓕ ⓢ c12000 81-12 GoodHpes,LionTmr,HppyDys 12
**FINISH** The horse finished first, a nose in front of the second horse. If second, third or unplaced, the superior figure indicates his margin behind the winner.

30Jun81–6AP 6f :22⁴ :46 1:11³ ft *6-5e 117⁵ 3³ 3² 2¹ 1ⁿᵒ SmithT³ ⓕ ⓢ c12000 81-12 GoodHpes,LionTmr,HppyDys 12
**JOCKEY AND POST POSITION** T. Smith rode the horse, who started from post position number 3

30Jun81–6AP 6f :22⁴ :46 1:11³ ft *6-5e 117⁵ 3³ 3² 2¹ 1ⁿᵒ SmithT³ ⓕ ⓢ c12000 81-12 GoodHpes,LionTmr,HppyDys 12
**CLAIMING PRICE OR TYPE OF RACE** The horse was entered to be claimed for $12,000 and the "c" indicates she was claimed, the ⓕ that the race was exclusively for fillies or fillies and mares, the ⓢ a restricted race that is not for open company. If it is an allowance race other than maiden or starter, the purse is given. If it is a stakes race, the name of the race is given.

30Jun81–6AP 6f :22⁴ :46 1:11³ ft *6-5e 117⁵ 3³ 3² 2¹ 1ⁿᵒ SmithT³ ⓕ ⓢ c12000 81-12 GoodHpes,LionTmr,HppyDys 12
**SPEED RATING** The horse's speed rating was 81

30Jun81–6AP 6f :22⁴ :46 1:11³ ft *6-5e 117⁵ 3³ 3² 2¹ 1ⁿᵒ SmithT³ ⓕ ⓢ c12000 81-12 GoodHpes,LionTmr,HppyDys 12
**TRACK VARIANT** The track variant that day was 12

30Jun81–6AP 6f :22⁴ :46 1:11³ ft *6-5e 117⁵ 3³ 3² 2¹ 1ⁿᵒ SmithT³ ⓕ ⓢ c12000 81-12 GoodHpes,LionTmr,HppyDys 12
**FIRST THREE FINISHERS** These are the first three finishers in the race

30Jun81–6AP 6f :22⁴ :46 1:11³ ft *6-5e 117⁵ 3³ 3² 2¹ 1ⁿᵒ SmithT³ ⓕ ⓢ c12000 81-12 GoodHpes,LionTmr,HppyDys 12
**NUMBER OF STARTERS** Twelve horses started in the race

races, the *pre-stretch call* refers to ¼ mile from the finish, or 3/16th miles from the finish, depending on the length of the stretch. The *mid-stretch call* refers to the eighth pole, or ⅛ mile from the finish. The *finish call* is the actual order of finish, provided by the photo-finish camera.

In the case of the 1¼-mile Kentucky Derby, for instance, the trackman must call the relative position for a 20-horse field at (a) the start, (b) the half-mile call, (c) the pre-stretch call (approximately one-fourth mile from the finish) and (d) the mid-stretch call. The relative finishing positions, with precise margins, would be provided by precisely calibrated cameras.

In a 5-furlong race, the trackman must call (a) the start, (b) the ¼ (c) the pre-stretch call and (d) the mid-stretch call. The finish will again be confirmed by the photo-finish camera, which is set up on the finish line at ground level.

It is exceedingly difficult to make an accurate race call. Consider the dilemma of calling 12 horses going 5 furlongs at 40 miles per hour or a 20-horse Kentucky Derby field traveling 1¼ miles. In the longer race, many horses are obscured from view, lost in the pack. In the shorter race, the trackman must pick up all the horses in three separate calls made during the first ⅜ of a mile, which takes about 35 seconds to run.

Daily Racing Form trackman Jack Wilson, who works in Florida during the winter and New York during the spring, summer and fall, hates the 5-furlong distance most of all, but he admitted last year that the toughest call he ever had to make was "the pre-stretch call of the 1983 Kentucky Derby." Wilson is the top trackman in the Daily Racing Form organization and annually calls the Triple Crown races on special assignment.

"There was a sudden rainstorm," Wilson recalled. "The sky turned so dark it was hard to see the field clearly on the backstretch. Then when the field turned the corner into the stretch, 20 horses fanned out as they usually do and it took all the concentration I have to pick them up as they headed toward me."

Wilson's chart may have caused him some anxious moments, but it was significantly more accurate than the chart produced by Sports Eye, a competing trade journal that has been producing racing charts at tracks throughout the country. To construct its 1983 Derby chart, Sports Eye had to rely on video-tape replays of the race.

Precise race-watching skills are an invaluable aid in handicapping. In fact, there is no higher skill to be acquired. Not only will the racing fan appreciate the race and see the inner workings of it more precisely, but he often will catch trackman mistakes, thus building an arsenal of useful data all his own.

The racing fan can help himself enormously by carefully observing the start, the turns and the final 1/16th of a mile. Video-tape replays are extremely useful when trying to see the inner workings of a fast-moving race, but the most important asset to bring to the task is a willingness to see more than the horse you bet. Lacking the time or the inclination to master objective race-watching skills, result charts should be saved and reviewed in depth.

Here is how these charts are created: While the race is in progress, the trackman describes the position of each horse to an assistant in a short-hand code. After the race, the trackman reviews the replays, double-checks the accuracy of his work, notes which horses were in traffic trouble or otherwise had interesting *trips*, adding fractional times supplied by the electronic timing gear, transmitting the completed chart to the home office.

For Canterbury Downs, these daily result charts will be transmitted to the Daily Racing Form, which will in turn transmit them to the Star and Tribune. The Star and Tribune will publish Daily Racing Form result charts the next day as part of our overall racing coverage.

At the Daily Racing Form, the information provided by these result charts is added to past performance profiles for every horse that has raced. These p.p.s include most of the new result chart information, but due to space limitations some information is deleted.

For example, in the Chicago edition of the Form, the start is not included in the past performance profile and the ¼-mile or ½-mile call also is dropped in p.p.s for races beyond a mile. When comparing result charts to p.p.s, it is important to realize that a result chart is a comprehensive source of information about one race, involving many horses, while the p.p. is a profile of one horse's career. But both are among the most intriguing statistical summaries in the world of sport.

# Could their performances have been predicted?

Proud Truth and Stephan's Odyssey ran 1-2 in February's Fountain of Youth Stakes at Gulfstream Park.

The two horses were the two top betting choices in the $100,000 stakes.

Stephan's Odyssey is owned by Henry DeKwiatkowski, trained by Woody Stephens. The jockey, not listed in Daily Racing Form past performances — but published in the official track program at Gulfstream Park — was Eddie Maple, a veteran stakes-class rider.

Proud Truth is owned by Dan Galbreath's Darby Dan Farm, trained by John Veitch, ridden by Jorge Velasquez; all are established veterans of stakes-class competition.

Let's examine each horse's lifetime racing record to see if their performances could have been predicted.

Stephan's Odyssey did not start his racing career until Oct. 21, 1984, rather late in the season for a Woody Stephens-trained 2-year-old (Perhaps there was a minor training injury?). In any case, the colt won his debut by 1¼ lengths, despite suffering a **bump** in an **11**-horse field. The bumping information appears beneath the p.p. line and the number 11 appears at the extreme right corner of the p.p. line. If we wished to find out more about it, we would need to review Oct. 21 result charts for Belmont Park. Good players know to keep files of daily result charts, even if they go racing only two or three times a month.

Other interesting tidbits mentioned in the Oct. 21 p.p. line include the **\*2-3** odds symbol that appears next to the weight information. The **\*** symbol designates a race favorite and the **2-3** means that a bet on Stephan's Odyssey was worth approximately $2 for every $3 wagered (If the betting odds are less than $1 for each dollar wagered, the horse is said to be an *odds-on favorite*).

It is unusual for a first-time starter to be so heavily bet. We must therefore surmise that Stephan's Odyssey had trained brilliantly for his racing debut and his victory suggests he may not need a recent race to produce a good performance.

Following a fourth-place finish at Aqueduct on Oct. 28, Stephan's Odyssey was next seen Dec. 2 at Hollywood Park, winning an allowance by a nose over Image of Greatness. The time, **1:09-3/5,** was 1/5 faster than the 6-furlong track record that existed before the start of the Hollywood Park meeting. These facts can be gleaned from the **101-05** figures that appear in the Dec. 2 p.p. line, alongside the class-of-race information, which is represented as **Aw22000** (An allowance race with a purse of $22,000).

The **101** is refered to as a **speed rating** or **speed figure**, and the **05** figure is the daily **track variant**. The Daily Racing Form computed these speed ratings and track variants by comparing final time clockings to the respective track records that were on the books at the start of the fall Hollywood meeting. Track records are assigned a speed rating of 100 points. Each 1/5 second slower or faster than the track record is worth one point (If a horse runs three full seconds slower than the track record, he will earn an 85 rating). The daily track variant is computed by averaging all winning times for a given day and then subtracting this average from 100. Thus, on Dec. 2, 1984, Stephan's Odyssey ran 1/5 of a second *faster* than the track record in his race; the average winning time for the entire day was one full second (5/5) *slower* than track record time.

The Daily Racing Form **speed figures** and **track variants** are rough approximations of what they purport to measure and are of limited use by handicappers. Far more sophisticated tools are needed to determine accurately how fast or slow the racetrack was on any given day.

With two victories in three sprints behind him, Stephan's Odyssey was next entered in the $1 million Hollywood Juvenile Championship at 1-1/16th miles Dec. 16, a very aggressive placement for such an inexperienced horse. Amazingly, the colt won that rich contest despite the fact he was making his first stakes appearance, his first try around two turns, his first race beyond a mile.

Now, two months later, for the colt's 1985 debut, trainer Stephens is choosing the Fountain of Youth stakes, another difficult assignment, and we must wonder why.

Why not a softer spot? Why not a race over the track against modest opposition before matching him against the best 3-year-olds in Florida? Can Stephan's Odyssey be ready for this race? Is he a seri-

## Stephan's Odyssey

Own.—DeKwiatkowski H

**122**

Dk. b. or br. c. 3, by Danzig—Kennelot, by Gallant Man
Br.—Kennelot Stables Ltd (Ky)     1984  4  3  0  0    $651,100
Tr.—Stephens Woodford C
Lifetime   4  3  0  0   $651,100

| | | | | | | | |
|---|---|---|---|---|---|---|---|
| 16Dec84–8Hol | 1$\frac{1}{16}$:45³ 1:10³ 1:43²gd | 11 121 | 10⁹ 42½ 11½ 1¹ | Maple E⁸ | Hol Futy | — — | Stphn'sOdyssy,FrstNormn,RghtCn 13 |
| 16Dec84–Grade I | | | | | | | |
| 2Dec84–3Hol | 6f :22 :45² 1:09³ft | 4 118 | 65½ 31½ 2hd 1no | Pincay L Jr¹ | Aw22000 | 101–05 | Stphn'sOdyssy,ImgofGrtnss,PrBwlr 6 |
| 28Oct84–6Aqu | 7f :22¹ :45 1:22³gd | *9-5 122 | 53¾ 31½ 3² 43½ | McCarron G³ | Aw20000 | 84–14 | AnotherReef,SecretaryGnrl,SkipTril 7 |
| 28Oct84–Drifted | | | | | | | |
| 21Oct84–6Bel | 6f :22⁴ :46² 1:12 ft | *2-3 118 | 4³ 32½ 2½ 11½ | Day P⁴ | Mdn | 82–21 | StphnsOdss,RllngMnstrl,DmscsSm 11 |
| 21Oct84–Bumped,clear | | | | | | | |

● Feb 16 Hia 4f ft :49 b     ● Feb 12 Hia 1 ft 1:40² b     ● Feb 7 Hia 6f ft 1:11 h     Feb 3 Hia 1 ft 1:42⁴ h

## Proud Truth

Own.—Darby Dan Farm

**112**

Ch. c. 3, by Graustark—Wake Robin, by Summer Tan
Br.—Galbreath Mrs J W (Ky)     1985  2  1  0  0    $20,337
Tr.—Veitch John M     1984  2  2  0  0    $18,000
Lifetime   4  3  0  0   $38,337

| | | | | | | | |
|---|---|---|---|---|---|---|---|
| 4Feb85–8GP | 1$\frac{1}{16}$:46³ 1:11³ 1:44²ft | *4-5 117 | 63½ 41½ 1¹ 1⁶ | Velasquez J² | Aw16000 | 79–18 | ProdTrth,CrownngHnrs,ScrtryGnrl 10 |
| 5Jan85–9Crc | 1$\frac{1}{16}$:48¹ 1:13 1:46³ft | *8-5 121 | 13¹⁶ 9¹⁵ 6⁸ 42¾ | VlsqzJ¹⁵ | Trop Pk Dby | 83–14 | Irish Sur, Artillerist, Banner Bob 16 |
| 5Jan85–Grade II | | | | | | | |
| 26Dec84–8Crc | 7f :22² :45⁴ 1:25¹ft | *1 119 | 77½ 5⁸ 52½ 1³ | Velasquez J¹ | Aw10000 | 90–22 | ProudTruth,Bowladrome,RegIBrek 12 |
| 26Dec84–BrkeInTangle,Clr | | | | | | | |
| 2Dec84–6Aqu | 6f :22⁴ :47 1:12²ft | 2e 118 | 84½ 76¾ 3¹ 12¾ | Velasquez J² | Mdn | 79–24 | Proud Truth,TakeControl,Buckner 10 |

Feb 12 Hia 4f ft :49 b     Feb 3 Hia 3f ft :36 b     ● Jan 29 Hia 6f ft 1:13² h     Jan 23 Hia 6f ft 1:14⁴ b

ous threat to win? To find out answers to these questions, we must consult the *workout line,* which is listed below the past performance profile. The workout line will tell us if this horse is or is not ready for a good race.

Observe that Stephan's Odyssey had two workouts at one mile each (Feb. 3 and Feb. 12) sandwiched around a very fast 6-furlong drill in **1:11** flat on Feb. 7. Note the positive effect of this 6-furlong workout. Note that the Feb. 12 mile was clocked in **1:40-2/5** breezing, which was *2-2/5 seconds faster* than the Feb. 3 workout, **1:42-4/5** handily (*Breezing* means without urging and *handily* means with mild use of the whip). The final workout, on Saturday, Feb. 16, was simply a 4-furlong breeze to put the colt on edge for his seasonal debut.

Proud Truth, on the other hand, also started his career with a winning debut late in the season (Dec. 2 at Aqueduct). But this is typical Veitch, typical Darby Dan procedure. In Proud Truth's case, he raced twice in December, once in January and once Feb. 4 at Gulfstream, winning at 1-1/16th miles by six lengths.

Observe that Proud Truth gained stakes experience in the 1 and 1/16-mile Tropical Park Derby on Jan. 5, finishing fourth, after making up 12 lengths in the final 3/16ths of a mile. Also, his workout line was irrelevant to his chances in the Fountain of Youth, although it was comforting to note he was out on the training track Feb. 12, eight days after his impressive recent victory. Clearly, this is a fit, improving 3-year-old who already has shown a fondness for 1-1/16 miles at Gulfstream Park.

The offical result confirmed what we have seen in the p.p.'s. Proud Truth beat Stephan's Odyssey by a neck after both horses rallied around most of the 14-horse field.

# Look carefully at this betting opportunity

The date is Dec. 26, 1984, and you're at the Fair Grounds race-track in New Orleans. It's the 11th race on the program and you're studying the past performances.

Look hard. Think carefully. There is an attractive, logical betting opportunity at hand.

Consider the eligibility conditions and the position of the start and finish as represented in the track diagram. In this case, the race is a $7,500 claiming event at 1-1/16 miles for 3-year-olds and up. This means we should not expect fit $10,000 or $15,000 horses in the field. Nor should we find maidens or allowance horses. If we do, we would have to question why.

Also, the stretch at the Fair Grounds is 1,346 feet, the longest in the United States. But the run to the first turn is slightly less than ⅛ mile, one of the shortest. There were 12 horses scheduled to compete and the illustration includes the five most accomplished contenders.

In post position No. 1 is **Essendeesbid,** who shows a win and a second in his last two starts. The trainer is Dwight Viator, ranked ninth in the trainer's standings, as published in the official track program. Jockey B.J. Walker, ranked third in the local standings, rode this horse in his last two starts and will ride again today.

In post position No. 2 is **Talkalittle Louder,** winner of his Fair Grounds debut Dec. 13 with jockey Randy Romero aboard. Romero set the Fair Grounds record for most wins during the previous winter meet. Trainer Frank Brothers is a perennial top 10 trainer at this track.

In post position No. 4 is **Western Buffalo**, dropping slightly in class after failing to finish in the money in his two most recent starts. During August and September, this horse was performing well in $10,000 to $12,000 claiming races in Kentucky. National riding champion Pat Day is the jockey. The trainer is Angel Barrera, nephew of Hall of Fame trainer Laz Barrera; the owner is Carmen Barrera, Laz's wife.

In post position No. 5 is **Exactly E.**, dropping sharply in class from the $20,000 claiming level. Jockey E.J. Perrodin is not in the top 20 and trainer Thad Ackel, ranked seventh at the current meet, is a steady, modestly successful owner-trainer on the Louisiana-Kentucky circuit.

In post position No. 12 is **Red Tammy,** a winner of 11 races, including a recent victory over similar opposition. The meet's leading trainer, Charles W. Walker, owns this horse and Jeff Faul, ranked fifth, replaces Ronald Ardoin in the saddle.

We now can begin to look at the key issues that will help determine a sensible selection:

■ Is there a horse that has an overpowering edge in ability? If so, is he in shape?

■ Is there a lone front-runner who might take an easy lead and take command of the race?

■ Are any horses compromised by their post position?

Observe that **Exactly E.** consistently has run with much superior opposition. Maybe he has a significant class advantage. If so, we must wonder why trainer Ackel is willing to drop this horse so sharply in claiming price. An answer to this question can be found in the dates column in the p.p.'s.

Exactly E.'s last race was Nov. 14, 1983, *more than a year ago.* He's a 6-year-old making his first 1984 start in late December. Also, his past performance profile shows only a single 4-furlong workout, hardly sufficient to prepare a horse for a 1 and 1/16-mile race. Exactly E. is not fit enough to race at peak form. If he was, Ackel would not be willing to sell him so cheaply. Exactly E. is a poor bet.

**Western Buffalo**'s main problem is his lack of early speed. He seldom gets out of his own way during the early stages and has only three wins in his last 34 starts. Most horses that lose contact with the early leaders seldom win. They need a hotly contested pace and terrific luck to avoid extremely wide trips or traffic problems. Western Buffalo must be regarded as a possible upsetter, but he will have to overcome his own sluggish beginning to enter serious contention.

Keep in mind the short run to the first turn. At the Fair Grounds, most 1 and 1/16-mile races are won by horses capable of breaking alertly to secure a good inside position. The long stretch may prove helpful to stretch-running horses such as Western Buffalo, but only

# 11th Fair Grounds

**1 1-16 MILES** FAIR GROUNDS START FINISH

**1 1/16 MILES. (1.42⅖) CLAIMING. Purse $5,000. 3-year-olds and upward. Weight, 3-year-olds, 119 lbs.; older, 121 lbs. Non-winners of two races since October 26 allowed 4 lbs.; a race since then, 7 lbs. Claiming price $7,500. (Claiming races for $6,500 or less not considered.)**

**Coupled—Ruggles Texan and Native Groogle.**

## Essendeesbid

**Own.—Folbe & Bobovich** **114**

**Ro. g. 5, by Delta Oil—Leah Lady, by Gaelic Gold**
**Br.—S & D Pottinger Inc (Ky)**
**Tr.—Viator Dwight J** **$7,500**
**Lifetime 42 8 11 4 $58,714**

| | | | | |
|---|---|---|---|---|
| 1984 | 17 | 3 4 1 | | $16,909 |
| 1983 | 15 | 5 2 1 | | $34,466 |
| Turf | 2 | 0 0 0 | | |

| | | | | | | | | | | | | | |
|---|---|---|---|---|---|---|---|---|---|---|---|---|---|
| 12Dec84-11FG | 140:484 1:143 1:432ft | 4¼ | 114 | 11½ | 11 | 2hd | 21 | Walker B J Jr2 | 7500 | 75-26 | RedTmmy,Essendeesbid,BlueCollr | 10 |
| 22Nov84-1FG | 1 1/16:481 1:134 1:47 ft | 8¼ | 114 | 21½ | 21 | 14 | 13 | Walker B J Jr11 | 5000 | 77-18 | Essndsbd,ExcponlRslts,YorFrdBll | 12 |
| 11Oct84-6JnD | 140:494 1:163 1:471gd | *8-5 | 115 | 32½ | 22 | 32½ | 513 | Munster L4 | 5000 | 49-34 | ArkieBaba,BodciousModred,TellPul | 8 |
| 12Aug84-1LaD | 7f :231 :464 1:26 ft | 4 | 118 | 52¾ | 73½ | 96½ | 911¼ | DelahoussayeDJ9 | 8000 | 83-12 | HighMagic,SandHillsRed,Acrodan | 12 |
| 28Jly84-1LaD | 170:47 1:124 1:443ft | 8 | 122 | 1hd | 2hd | 31½ | 75½ | DelahoussayeDJ8 | 8000 | 68-16 | HappyJim,RealTwister,WhtADrive | 11 |
| 11Jly84-7LaD | 170:463 1:113 1:412ft | 6½ | 114 | 21½ | 4nk | 74¾ | 911¾ | Frazier R L6 | 12500 | 78-14 | Prince Raj, Nickle Bidder, Rastic | 9 |
| 30Jun84-1LaD | 170:474 1:122 1:424ft | 6 | 114 | 1½ | 12 | 15 | 14 | DelahoussyeDJ11 | 8000 | 83-07 | Essndsbd,OccsonlyMondy,Doc'sPc | 12 |
| 6Jun84-2LaD | 7f :233 :471 1:262gd | 4½ | 114 | 53½ | 43½ | 42 | 23½ | DelahoussyeDJ11 | 8000 | 88-19 | MronConty,Essndsbd,OnBoldScot | 12 |
| 26May84-2LaD | 6f :222 :454 1:104ft | 21 | 114 | 86½ | 55 | 44 | 26 | DelahoussayeDJ9 | 8000 | 83-09 | Rastic, Essendeesbid,TwoFeathers | 12 |
| 28Mar84-11FG | 1 1/16:474 1:143 1:473ft | 2½ | 116 | 2½ | 57 | 817 | 826¾ | Shubert R C8 | c7500 | 47-22 | BggrBuck,BttrThnBucks,RunEsyRn | 8 |

**Dec 22 FG 4f ft :51 b    Dec 8 FG 3f ft :38 b    Nov 21 FG 3f ft :37 b**

## Talkalittle Louder

**Own.—Franks J** **114**

**Dk. b. or br. c. 4, by Tell—Ionic Miss, by My Dad George**
**Br.—Gibbsleigh Farms (Ill)**
**Tr.—Brothers Frank L** **$7,500**
**Lifetime 16 5 4 1 $54,984**

| | | | | |
|---|---|---|---|---|
| 1984 | 6 | 1 1 0 | | $4,372 |
| 1983 | 7 | 3 2 1 | | $25,550 |

| | | | | | | | | | | | | | |
|---|---|---|---|---|---|---|---|---|---|---|---|---|---|
| 13Dec84-1FG | 1 1/16:471 1:13 1:454ft | 2½ | 114 | 1hd | 1hd | 11½ | 12 | Romero R P3 | 5000 | 83-19 | TlklttlLdr,ArctcThndr,ExcpnlRslts | 12 |
| 2Dec84-1LaD | 170:471 1:13 1:44 ft | 3½ | 114 | 11 | 1hd | 21 | 25 | Ardoin R6 | 8000 | 72-21 | NtiveGroogle,TlklittleLouder,ArilL | 12 |
| 16Nov84-5LaD | 6f :231 :472 1:124ft | *2½ | 114 | 63½ | 108¼ | 77 | 57½ | Whited D E7 | 8000 | 71-18 | StlIngot,WorldEmpror,CountDsty | 12 |
| 7Oct84-3LaD | 7f :224 :463 1:264m | *1 | 114 | 2hd | 44 | 710 | 713 | Romero R P7 | 8000 | 77-16 | WhatADrive,YourHlf,HveANiceDy | 10 |
| 14Sep84-5LaD | 7f :224 :454 1:242ft | *2 | 114 | 1hd | 3½ | 32 | 53½ | Romero R P6 | 12500 | 98-16 | NickleBidder,BllStppr,JustinScott | 12 |
| 1Sep84-7LaD | 6f :222 :453 1:11 ft | 4 | 116 | 2hd | 2hd | 2hd | 53¼ | Snyder L2 | 16000 | 85-10 | Iron Hawk, DustinPower,StarTrap | 10 |
| 7Aug83-5LaD | 6½f :23 :474 1:212ft | *8-5 | 116 | 22 | 34½ | 47 | 511 | Perrodin E J7 | 32000 | 57-32 | Tudor Tuff,Hempen'sGuy,Profanity | 8 |
| 24Jly83-6LaD | 6½f :224 :46 1:183ft | *1 | 116 | 5¾ | 53¼ | 43½ | 32 | Snyder L1 | 32000 | 80-22 | BunnyPack,Activus,TlklittleLouder | 6 |
| 16Jun83-6LaD | 170:472 1:123 1:441ft | *8-5 | 114 | 1hd | 1½ | 1½ | 1no | Snyder L4 | 40000 | 76-22 | TlklittleLouder,OvernitSuccss,Coitr | 7 |
| 22May83-8LaD | 6½f :231 :472 1:224m | *6-5 | 116 | 2½ | 33½ | 31½ | 1½ | Snyder L4 | 32000 | 61-35 | TlklittlLoudr,Officr'sMss,GnnGFstr | 9 |

**Nov 4 LaD 5f gd 1:01 h**

## Western Buffalo

**Own.—Barrera C S** **114**

**B. h. 6, by Buffalo Lark—Western Idol, by Western Sky II**
**Br.—Morgan Nancy Penn (Ky)**
**Tr.—Barrera Angel** **$7,500**
**Lifetime 78 8 9 9 $81,957**

| | | | | |
|---|---|---|---|---|
| 1984 | 20 | 2 2 3 | | $12,835 |
| 1983 | 14 | 1 3 0 | | $12,248 |
| Turf | 22 | 2 3 1 | | $24,065 |

| | | | | | | | | | | | | | |
|---|---|---|---|---|---|---|---|---|---|---|---|---|---|
| 14Dec84-5FG | a1 1/16 (T):482 1:133 1:462fm | 22 | 114 | 910 | 118½ | 87½ | 74¾ | Oliva L Jr9 | 10000 | 75-20 | BeeSeven,NowandThen,NtiveBurn | 12 |
| 23Nov84-10FG | 1 1/16:482 1:134 1:463ft | 14 | 114 | 1011 | 1011 | 911 | 97¾ | Oliva L Jr9 | 10000 | 71-20 | Georgealite,RelTwister,Fleetmore | 11 |
| 19Oct84-8Kee | 1 1/16:474 1:131 1:46 ft | 13 | 115 | 1018 | 86 | 510 | 511¼ | Agnello A3 | 15000 | 65-20 | Bal Bay, Piasa, Really Silver | 12 |
| 30Sep84-8Lat | 1 1/16:474 1:124 1:471ft | 6½ | 115 | 1011 | 87¾ | 72¾ | 2¾ | Agnello A3 | 12500 | 73-23 | Ad'sKnight,WestrnBufflo,RllySilvr | 10 |
| 20Sep84-8Lat | 1 1/16:472 1:124 1:461ft | *2½ | 115 | 714 | 53½ | 2½ | 11½ | Agnello A4 | 10000 | 79-28 | WstrnBfflo,CrowNton,Bob'sJncton | 8 |
| 31Aug84-5CD | 1 1/16:481 1:132 1:462ft | 8½ | 116 | 69 | 65½ | 32½ | 41¼ | Melancon L1 | 11000 | 75-18 | Copula, Tom Lightfoot,J.KittyKitty | 8 |
| 21Aug84-8CD | 1 1/16:482 1:13 1:464ft | 8½ | 115 | 611 | 66 | 43 | 3¾ | Haire D2 | 10000 | 73-17 | PocktfllOfHp,PrvtAngsh,WstrnBffl | 7 |
| 18Jly84-8CD | 1 1/16:482 1:132 1:453ft | 7½ | 112 | 712 | 66½ | 47 | 45¼ | Melancon L4 | 10000 | 75-12 | Wiltinger,BrillintB.,BoldApprentice | 8 |
| 6Jly84-8CD | 1 1/16:491 1:14 1:463sy | 18 | 112 | 912 | 87½ | 75¾ | 35 | Melancon L9 | 10000 | 70-16 | Hrrno,PopcornCssrol,WstrnBufflo | 10 |
| 27Jun84-5CD | 1 1/8:491 1:142 1:553ft | 70 | 112 | 65¼ | 66 | 67½ | 67¼ | Melancon L3 | 12500 | 57-24 | Credentialed, Wiltinger, Herreno | 6 |

**Dec 8 FG 4f ft :491 b**

## Exactly E. *

**Own.—Ackel G J** **114**

**Dk. b. or br. h. 6, by Verbatim—Good Groomer, by Bold Bidder**
**Br.—Tackett P & R (Ky)**
**Tr.—Ackel Thad D** **$7,500**
**Lifetime 26 7 4 3 $63,476**

| | | | | |
|---|---|---|---|---|
| 1983 | 11 | 3 3 2 | | $26,305 |
| 1982 | 4 | 1 0 0 | | $9,634 |
| Turf | 4 | 0 0 1 | | $2,022 |

| | | | | | | | | | | | | | |
|---|---|---|---|---|---|---|---|---|---|---|---|---|---|
| 14Nov83-9CD | 1 1/16:472 1:123 1:462ft | *4-5e | 112 | 1012 | 912 | 65½ | 42 | Day P3 | 20000 | 74-23 | Harpers Bazaar,Mr.Bobeva,Supron | 10 |
| 14Nov83—Threw his head at the start | | | | | | | | | | | | |
| 14Aug83-7LaD | a1 1/16 (T):47 1:113 1:424fm | 9 | 116 | 2hd | 1hd | 4nk | 76¼ | Perrodin E J4 | 40000 | 83-11 | StrightStr,BrkrBrkr,NorthrnRockt | 12 |
| 31Jly83-6LaD | 1 1/16:474 1:122 1:434ft | *3-2 | 1115 | 1½ | 1½ | 21½ | 24 | Valovich C J6 | 40000 | 89-13 | WorthyAntgonst,ExctlyE.,Mr'sPlsr | 6 |
| 10Jly83-7LaD | 1 1/16:464 1:12 1:45 ft | 2 | 1175 | 1hd | 1hd | 31 | 44¾ | Valovich C J2 | Aw15000 | 82-15 | Dr. Spanky, Ringgold, Navajo Trail | 6 |
| 26Jun83-6LaD | 1 1/16:472 1:124 1:46 m | *1 | 119 | 1hd | 12½ | 18 | 19 | Ardoin R3 | A16000 | 82-25 | Exactly E.,WardKeeper,NativeBurn | 9 |
| 29May83-10LaD | 1 (T):463 1:111 1:362fm | 4½ | 116 | 21½ | 2hd | 1hd | 31½ | Ardoin R4 | 40000 | 90-09 | BrekerBrkr,RunforthMstr,ExctlyE. | 11 |
| 18May83-6CD | 1 1/16:483 1:132 1:443sy | *1 | 117 | 14 | 12 | 15 | 15 | Day P2 | 27500 | 85-17 | Exactly E., Foundation, Major Run | 6 |
| 6May83-4CD | 1 1/8:482 1:123 1:493ft | 2½ | 117 | 23 | 21½ | 2½ | 22½ | Hawley S4 | 25000 | 91-15 | Top Brick, Exactly E., Dual Tracks | 6 |
| 17Feb83-8FG | 1 1/16:474 1:123 1:451ft | *1 | 113 | 21½ | 2hd | 11½ | 15½ | Ardoin R6 | c17500 | 86-22 | ExactlyE.,Mam'sBrother,MisterGuy | 7 |
| 10Feb83-10FG | 1 1/16:481 1:133 1:452gd | *9-5e | 115 | 1hd | 1½ | 1hd | 32¾ | Ardoin R3 | 20000 | 82-22 | Princely Verdict, Cabby,ExactlyE. | 10 |

**Dec 21 FG 4f ft :484 b**

## Red Tammy

**Own.—Walker C W** **117**

**Ro. g. 7, by Red Charmer—Tammy Tam, by Our Tammy**
**Br.—Richmond, E W (Ky)**
**Tr.—Walker Charles W** **$7,500**
**Lifetime 70 11 8 13 $140,885**

| | | | | |
|---|---|---|---|---|
| 1984 | 17 | 3 2 2 | | $21,166 |
| 1983 | 15 | 0 2 0 | | $9,594 |
| Turf | 23 | 2 2 5 | | $39,461 |

| | | | | | | | | | | | | | |
|---|---|---|---|---|---|---|---|---|---|---|---|---|---|
| 12Dec84-11FG | 140:484 1:143 1:432ft | *3-2 | 117 | 32½ | 21 | 1hd | 11 | Ardoin R5 | 7500 | 76-26 | RedTmmy,Essendeesbid,BlueCollr | 10 |
| 30Nov84-4FG | 1 1/16:484 1:141 1:47 sl | 3e | 114 | 64 | 31 | 1½ | 31½ | Faul J H2 | 10000 | 75-23 | Keno Hill, Real Twister,RedTammy | 9 |
| 20Oct84-5LaD | 170:474 1:144 1:471sy | 3¾ | 114 | 1014 | 612 | 515 | 316 | SteinbrgPW10 | c10000 | 45-35 | PrincelyVerdict,RlTwistr,RdTmmy | 11 |
| 13Oct84-1LaD | 170:472 1:143 1:47 m | *6-5 | 114 | 89½ | 43½ | 11½ | 11½ | Lively J2 | 8000 | 62-24 | Red Tammy, Indio Jo, Semi Beau | 11 |
| 9Sep84-7LaD | 170:472 1:113 1:414ft | *2½ | 119 | 42 | 63¾ | 65½ | 65½ | Lively J7 | 16000 | 82-14 | BrazeandBold,NaturlFlir,Weququet | 7 |
| 19Aug84-5LaD | 170:461 1:114 1:422ft | 4¾ | 122 | 914 | 87 | 55 | 2nk | Whited D E1 | 16000 | 85-11 | PrinceRj,RdTmmy,Imp'sChosunSon | 9 |
| 4Aug84-5LaD | 170:473 1:124 1:451gd | 4 | 116 | 67½ | 46½ | 26 | 12½ | Lively J7 | 16000 | 71-30 | RedTammy,BellStepper,PrinceRaj | 11 |
| 21Jly84-5LaD | 170:464 1:124 1:44 ft | 9¾ | 116 | 96¾ | 87 | 94¾ | 41½ | Lively J9 | 16000 | 75-17 | Sissy'sAgitation,Topach,Shogunte | 12 |
| 3Jun84-11LaD | 7f :23 :454 1:233ft | 43 | 114 | 116¼ | 97 | 106¾ | 99 | Lively J8 | 25000 | 97-08 | Tolerble,WhippedCrem,NlesRockt | 12 |
| 5Mar84-12FG | 1 1/8:481 1:13 1:513ft | 3 | 114 | 43 | 21 | 31 | 41½ | Day P6 | 25000 | 84-18 | Big'NBeutiful,IronTerri,Ky'sBnquet | 8 |

**Nov 21 FG 5f ft 1:041 b**

if the leaders recklessly duel each other into submission.

**Essendeesbid, Talkalittle Louder** and **Red Tammy** have similar records and styles. All have sufficient speed to race with or near the leaders and thus may combine to create the kind of speed duel Western Buffalo needs to win. But another scenario is probable.

Red Tammy is facing a tough task. Breaking from post 12, he will have to lose ground in the run around the first turn. He has speed but is unlikely to outbreak the two speed horses sitting in posts one and two.

Essendeesbid and Talkalittle Louder both have won races over this track during the past month. Both have good early speed and inside post positions. Talkalittle Louder won his most recent race wire to wire at the $5,000 claiming level. Essendeesbid won for $5,000 two races back and was a good second to Red Tammy in a $7,500 race Dec. 12.

If both horses engage in a speed duel, they might damage each other's winning chances, but a few clues in the past performances say this is not likely to happen. Essendeesbid won his Nov. 22 race from post 11, showing good speed and overcoming a front-runner to draw away by three lengths. This speaks well for his early and middle race speed, the speed he will need to defeat Talkalittle Louder during the first half of the race. Furthermore, in his recent second-place finish to Red Tammy, he showed more front-running speed than any race since June, a sign of present sharpness, a sign confirmed by two workouts sandwiched around his Dec. 12 race. Few claiming horses are so active on the training track (Compare his workout line with all the others in this race). This is a very fit horse with the coveted No. 1 post at a distance that favors inside running positions. If Essendeesbid doesn't break into a clear lead early, he has the speed to shake loose midway through the race. At the very least, he is a solid contender.

Talkalittle Louder obviously is fast enough to win and may prove best. But his overall health is suspect. During the past two years, he has raced only 13 times and as a former $30,000 claimer, it is interesting to note that no trainer bothered to claim him while he was descending the claiming ladder. Talkalittle Louder is a possible winner but hardly a bargain at 8-5 odds, not unless he can outrace Essendeesbid for the lead and the rail, which is highly questionable.

The race ran true to form. Essendeesbid took a narrow lead from Talkalittle Louder and stretched his advantage to three lengths entering the final turn to coast to a 2½-length victory. Talkalittle Louder faded back to 10th. Red Tammy rallied wide for second and Western Buffalo made a mild rally but flattened out to finish fourth. Exactly E. showed a little early speed before fading to 11th.

# Four steps to building a winning approach

We have been exploring the finer points of handicapping, reading Daily Racing Form past performance profiles, learning the language of the sport and making predictions.

We examined the p.p.'s of Proud Truth and Stephan's Odyssey as they appeared for the Fountain of Youth Stakes on Feb. 18 and compared the racing records of five horses in a $7,500 claiming racethat took place Dec. 26 at the Fair Grounds.

The analytical process was the same for each horse, in both races. Our objective was to determine if the horse was (a) properly placed in the race, (b) fit, or of questionable fitness, (c) suited to the probable pace of the race, (d) advantaged or disadvantaged by running style or post position.

To find answers to these questions, it is helpful to develop a procedure that will steer us in the right direction. The past performance profile contains many tidbits of information and it can be perplexing trying to figure out what to look for first.

What follows is a recapitulation of some important considerations, the foundation for a sound handicapping method. The intent is *not* to provide a *system* to pick winners, nor an ironclad list of DO's and DON'T's. This is just a starting point from which players may begin to develop their own approach to the sport, an approach that should be based on one's own particular strengths.

**One/ Eliminate scratches, make appropriate jockey changes and note the final post position assignments as published in the official track program.** The Daily Racing Form past performances do not include such information for today's race.

**Two/ Read the conditions of eligibility for the race in question and consider the position of the starting gate relative to the first turn involved.**

If the configuration of the track or other factors (i.e. strong head-winds, or mud, etc.) cause a bias for or against specific running styles or post positions, the player should have the same bias before eliminating or upgrading potential contenders.

At Canterbury Downs, watch the start and the turns of all races. Analyze and save yesterday's result charts.

Biases exist at all tracks, but they sometimes shift according to weather conditions and track maintenance. Keep in mind that few horses win against severe post-position biases, or running style tendencies. Those that overcome such problems deserve respect in the future, perhaps in better class races.

**Three/ Identify horses dropping sharply in class.**

Take a close look at the recent racing record or workout line. Is the horse suspiciously placed here? Is today's claiming price or class of race a fair estimate of this horse's worth, or is it simply a signal that the trainer is discouraged and willing to sell the horse cheaply? Knowledge of the trainer and his methods will take much of the guesswork out of such inquiries.

To acquire that knowledge, the player may need to compare a half-dozen past performance examples of one particular trainer, observing the way he handled each horse. Did his dropdowns win or fail to enter contention? Most trainers tend to rely on previously successful patterns. These patterns can be gleaned from past performance profiles.

Players at Canterbury Downs should consider keeping a notebook on trainers.

Develop a system of giving credit to trainers who win with first-time starters, or dropdowns, or horses that have not raced in several months.

Give extra credit to trainers who win first out with newly claimed horses and don't overlook trainers who win races beyond a mile with sprinters stretching out in distance.

**Four/ Read each past performance profile to determine the intention of the trainer with respect to today's race.**

Is the horse young and inexperienced? Is the trainer moving it forward toward a winning goal? Is the horse a veteran? Is the trainer entering it in a race that suits the horse's known talents?

No prior knowledge of trainer's methods is required to form a practical opinion on the trainer's overall game plan for the horse. Judge for yourself if the trainer seems to have a plan, or if he doesn't seem to be in control of the situation.

At Canterbury, the vast majority of players will not have handicapping experience or knowledge of trainers. But no experience is required to formulate a judgment based on common sense. Believe it or not, common sense is the one indispensable ingredient in a sound handicapping method. In fact, there is no better tool of logic to be utilized.

Although luck is always a factor in individual races, race results are not the product of pure chance. The best trainers and jockeys win more often than their rivals; the best horses win more races and more money at higher levels of competition. Developing a sound handicapping approach means the willingness to inquire in a logical manner, utilizing the tools at hand, creating new ones if necessary. It may seem an oversimplification, but consider this: Becoming a successful lawyer, doctor, teacher or writer requires the same willingness to learn.

# Watching races on TV helps build insight

One of the best ways to learn about thoroughbred racing is to follow the Triple Crown chase and other major stakes televised throughout the year.

We see the best horses, jockeys and trainers competing for millions of dollars and can follow their progress from one race to the next. The cameras occasionally peek in on how a colt is raised, broken and prepared for his first breeze around the track. Or perhaps we will see the way a race looked from different angles, or why and how a foul was committed.

Last year on the excellent Breeders' Cup telecast, viewers were right alongside the Hollywood Park stewards when they disqualified Gate Dancer from second to third and disallowed the claim of foul against the winner, Wild Again.

In some ways, watching races in person is harder than watching on television. Television makes decisions for us, moves closer to the action and gives us a few different angles or replays to confirm or alter our original impressions.

Not that television always does a great job. It often fails to spend enough time with the most significant part of the telecast, *the race itself.* On most broadcasts, post time usually is 15 or 20 minutes before sign-off. This is barely time enough to present the race and one replay. These are precious moments worth careful attention. Sometimes the best horse was trapped in a pocket, as Little Current was in the 1974 Kentucky Derby, when he finished fifth in a 23-horse field, the largest in Derby history.

In the Preakness two weeks later, the same horse hugged the

rail and sailed past the field in the stretch.

In the 1983 Blue Grass Stakes, the favorite, Marfa, lugged in on Desert Wine, causing jockey Sandy Hawley to stand up in his irons, losing all chance. For some strange reason, the Churchill Downs crowd made Marfa the favorite for the 1983 Kentucky Derby, even though trainer Wayne Lukas said on TV and in the press that the horse would be kept extremely wide to temper Marfa's roughish behavior.

In the Derby, long-shot Desert Wine set the pace to finish second to Sunny's Halo as Marfa appeared to be rallying from the parking lot. Alert TV viewers might have noticed an incident in deep stretch that involved Marfa and future champion Slew o' Gold.

Slew o' Gold had run very well to make a serious challenge in mid-stretch, but he obviously was not mature enough to win a classic race and grudgingly gave ground to the leaders inside the final ⅛ mile.

Then along came Marfa, who leaned in on Slew o' Gold while taking over fourth position. But, somehow, the young son of Seattle Slew found one last burst of energy to retake fourth at the wire.

Fourth place isn't anything to write home about, even in the Kentucky Derby. But in Slew o' Gold's case it showed unusual courage. If you set your mind to notice such things, you will build insight upon insight without needing the Racing Form or a thousand hours of study.

# The Florida Derby
# of 1985

Just as we learned many things from the 1984 Flamingo Stakes, there was much to be learned from watching the 1985 Florida Derby.

Despite the mediocre time for the 1⅛th-mile distance, 1:50 flat, the winner, Proud Truth, ran an *interesting* race, one that confirmed his credentials as a top-quality colt, a contender for the Triple Crown races.

This could be seen by the way he accelerated between horses in the final eighth mile. The colt put in a fine burst of speed when the race was on the line.

As seen on TV or through binoculars in the grandstand, jockey Jorge Velasquez had struggled to get Proud Truth to respond for most of the first mile, but nothing Velasquez did seemed to work. The colt was not running smoothly.

With about ⅜ of a mile to go, Velasquez reached down with the whip and hit Proud Truth at least five fimes trying to remind the colt that this was an important race. But Proud Truth didn't respond. He moved a bit closer to the leaders — Mighty Appealing and Covert Operation — but only because he was obviously better than most of his rivals and because he was saving as much ground as possible along the rail.

Turning into the stretch, Proud Truth still was five lengths behind Banner Bob as the latter moved quickly from third to first to assume a two-length lead in the upper stretch. Meanwhile, Irish Sur had begun to uncork a sustained run from the far outside to loom a bold factor.

If you were watching the race carefully, you might have seen everything change quickly inside the final ⅛ mile.

Irish Sur continued his rally, taking a slight lead from Banner Bob, and appeared to be on his way to victory. Proud Truth still was three lengths behind the top pair and trapped inside of the tiring Covert Operation. Velasquez was still working the whip, trying to get Proud Truth into the race. Suddenly an opening developed as the leaders edged closer to the finish. Velasquez reacted instantly. So did Proud Truth.

If you appreciate good athletes — whether they have two or four legs — you would have liked what Velasquez and Proud Truth did in the final drive to the wire in this $300,000 contest.

In a flash, Velasquez pointed Proud Truth toward the narrow opening, bumping Covert Operation soundly to secure more running room, a borderline foul that might have brought disqualification had the victim not been in retreat.

Suddenly, Proud Truth accelerated into his best clip to assert his superiority. Irish Sur was moving strongly, but Proud Truth made him look like he was tied to a post.

Although Proud Truth's clocking was only the 19th-fastest ever recorded in the 34-year history of the Florida Derby, his final ⅛ mile (12-2/5 seconds) was well above average and his final 1/16th was among the best ever. (Proud Truth was three lengths behind the leader at the ⅛ pole). Using interpolation and comparing the colt's position to the fractional times, Proud Truth's final 1/16th of a mile was clocked in 6 seconds flat — a superior burst of late speed in the colt's first try at a race this distance.

The splits read as follows: The first quarter mile in 23-3/5, the half in 47-3/5, three-quarters in 1:11-3/5, a mile in 1:37 flat and the final clocking in 1:50.)

That's a finishing punch worthy of a good horse, especially one who still was learning what the game is all about.

As for the rest of the field, including the favorite Stephan's Odyssey, here is a thumbnail sketch of what we should file away for the future.

**Irish Sur/** Made a wide move and proved he is a legitimate stakes horse, one that may also like the classic distances.

**Do It Again Dan/** Closed well for third despite some traffic problems in the upper stretch. Although unable to win in this company yet, he has put in several honest performances and deserves a chance to figure in the Triple Crown chase.

**Banner Bob/** Had the benefit of a slow pace and took command at the proper time only to lose his best stride in the final furlong. *Definitely not* a Derby horse, but a top-class sprinter who has been stretched out as far as he wants to go.

**Covert Operation/** Gave a good try from the extreme outside post and was bothered by the winner while tiring slightly. A good performance by an underrated horse. Not a Derby threat but a colt with stakes-class talent.

**Stephan's Odyssey/** Raced well for the first mile but failed to enter contention when it counted. This failure to improve off his good second to Proud Truth in the Fountain of Youth Stakes confirmed an old Woody Stephens pattern. The Hall of Fame trainer is an expert at getting horses ready for a top race after a layoff but frequently his horses fail to fire in their next races.

Because the Fountain of Youth was Stephan's Odyssey's first race in two months and it proved to be such a difficult assignment, it apparently cost him some strength as he attempted to stretch out to 1⅛ miles for the first time in his life. The verdict is still out on this colt — he may not like 1¼ miles — but we should reserve final judgment on his Derby credentials until his next appearance.

Of the rest, only **Mighty Appealing**, who tired badly to finish 10th, made any impression in the contest. This is a fine horse, the winner of two major stakes last season, but he has not shown much in three Florida races. Trainer Dean Gaudet should consider taking her pride and joy back to Maryland, where she might be able to set a new schedule for the Preakness. So far the colt has not displayed anything close to his 1984 form.

# Speed vs. class/
# A continuing debate

In politics, there is the perennial debate between liberals and conservatives. In economics, it's capitalism vs. socialism. In horse-race handicapping, its *speed* vs. *class.*

Most handicappers fall in one camp or the other, even though neither by itself explains the complexities of the sport.

Let's define both philosophical terms as they are used by their proponents.

A *class* handicapper labels the horse according to its racing record.

A *speed* handicapper, also known as a *speed figure* handicapper, considers time the ultimate measure of ability and pays almost no attention to the class of race.

Where class handicappers tend to select horses that have raced against better opposition, speed handicappers tend to bet horses that have run faster races.

For a class handicapper, a $10,000 claimer is a horse that has been competing in $10,000 races. A stakes horse is a horse that has been meeting other stakes horses.

For the speed handicapper, there is no such thing as class. He thinks only in terms of actual results and the realities of the tele-timer. The speed handicapper demands that the horse prove its supposed class by running faster than its rivals.

A speed handicapper expects victory from a horse capable of running 1:10 over one that has been running 1:10-3/5. This expectation is just as strong if the slower horse has been racing against classier rivals.

## Aqueduct Parallel Time Chart

| Claiming class | Speed figure | Six furlongs | Seven furlongs | One mile (One turn) | 1½ mile (Two turns) |
|---|---|---|---|---|---|
| $75,000 | 116 | 1:10 2/5 | 1:23 | 1:35 4/5 | 1:50 1/5 |
| $50,000 | 112 | 1:10 3/5 | 1:23 2/5 | 1:36 1/5 | 1:50 4/5 |
| $35,000 | 108 | 1:11 | 1:23 4/5 | 1:36 3/5 | 1:51 1/5 |
| $25,000 | 104 | 1:11 1/5 | 1:24 1/5 | 1:37 | 1:52 4/5 |
| $20,000 | 100 | 1:11 3/5 | 1:24 3/5 | 1:37 3/5 | 1:52 1/5 |
| $15,000 | 96 | 1:11 4/5 | 1:24 4/5 | 1:37 4/5 | 1:52 3/5 |
| $12,500 | 92 | 1:12 1/5 | 1:25 1/5 | 1:38 1/5 | 1:53 |
| $10,000 | 88 | 1:12 2/5 | 1:25 2/5 | 1:38 3/5 | 1:53 2/5 |

A drop in class is meaningless to the speed handicapper, while the class handicapper expects slower horses to improve when trainers drop them into cheaper races.

Not withstanding this arcane view of speed and class that has been reinforced by numerous authors of books on handicapping, the differences between the schools of thought are mostly illusion.

Examine the relationship between time and class in the accompanying chart. The speed purist must construct a chart such as this to make valid time comparisons. The figures in this parallel time chart were generated by averaging the final times of hundreds of races at every class level at every distance. The chart is the result of hundreds of hours of research.

At Aqueduct, for instance, the chart shows that the *class par* for a $25,000 claiming race at six furlongs is 1:11-1/5. At seven furlongs, the same class of horses average 1:24-1/5.

Deeper reading of this chart will reveal that both of these final times equal a 104 *speed figure* despite the fact that they were recorded at different distances. (The speed figure portion of the chart was generated by assigning 100 to the $20,000 claiming class and it takes into account the difference in speed measured by each 1/5th of a second.)

Remember, these class pars were produced by averaging the final times of thousands of races at each class level. Thus, $50,000 claimers at Aqueduct probably will run six furlongs in 1:10-3/5 on a normal fast track.

But what if they don't? What if a $50,000 claiming race is run in 1:09 flat? Wouldn't we have to conclude that the winner is a *classier* animal or can it be that the speed of the track contributed to the clocking?

Maybe the answer is a little of both and maybe we need to look at other races run the same day to properly evaluate the situation. Therein lies the beginning thought behind successful **speed figure handicapping,** which obviously incorporates notions about class into the handicapping equation.

If all nine races on a single day are clocked one second faster than par, the speed figure handicapper knows that the track itself probably was responsible for the faster than usual clockings.

If all nine races average out to be 1-3/5 seconds slow or 1/5th second slow, the speed figure handicapper knows that a winning horse clocked two seconds faster than the daily average is worth remembering. Such a horse probably is capable of moving up in class for his next winning assignment.

When a speed figure handicapper takes note of the times for all races on a single card, he compares them with the par times and averages the difference. This difference is called the *track variant.*

By way of example, when the great horse Secretariat won the 1973 Belmont Stakes, he set a world record of 2:24 flat for the 1½ miles. The rest of the day produced eight clockings that were only 1 second faster than par for all other classes and distances. Secretariat's race was 4-3/5 seconds faster than the typical Belmont, thus earning him an adjusted speed figure of 141, the highest on record at any distance at any track.

# The speed of the track, the speed of the race

The parallel time chart we are using is based on private research. It has nothing to do with Daily Racing Form speed ratings, which are based on track records. There are fundamental flaws built into Daily Racing Form speed ratings, some of which undermine their value.

Compare the Aqueduct track records. Note that the difference between the 6-furlong and 7-furlong record is 12 seconds and the difference between 7 furlongs and one mile (8 furlongs) is 13 seconds. While the track records show the horse can be expected to slow at the longer distance, there is something out of whack. The difference is too great; 13 seconds is too big a gap to explain; the Aqueduct mile mark is *not in parallel* with the 7-furlong record.

The reason for this reflects a fundamental reality at Aqueduct. The mile record is *slower* than it should be because at Aqueduct fewer stakes races are run at one mile than at 6 or 7 furlongs. This means fewer fast horses get the opportunity to set a true one-mile record. (Using the 6 and 7-furlong records as a reasonable standard, the one-mile mark should be 1:32-2/5.)

With a built-in error factor of 4/5 of a second at one mile, Aqueduct track records are not a sound measuring stick in a game where a length equals about 1/5 of a second and a neck or a nose can mean the difference between victory or defeat. Similar error factors exist at one or more distances at most other tracks.

The error factor is compounded by Daily Racing Form track variants, which are computed by comparing all clockings on a single

# Time Records vs.
# The Parallel Time Chart

## Aqueduct Time Records

| Distance | Horse | Age | Wgt. | Time | Date |
|----------|-------|-----|------|------|------|
| 6 furlongs | Dave's Friend | 5 | 126 | 1:08 1/5 | Nov. 29, 1980 |
| 7 furlongs | Dr. Fager | 4 | 139 | 1:20 1/5 | Nov. 2, 1968 |
| 1 mile | Florage | 5 | 116 | 1:33 1/5 | July 16, 1974 |
| 1⅛ miles | Riva Ridge | 4 | 130 | 1:40 | Oct. 15, 1973 |

## Aqueduct Parallel Time Chart

| Claiming class | Speed figure | Six furlongs | Seven furlongs | One mile (One turn) | 1½ mile (Two turns) |
|----------------|--------------|--------------|----------------|---------------------|---------------------|
| $75,000 | 116 | 1:10 2/5 | 1:23 | 1:35 4/5 | 1:50 1/5 |
| $50,000 | 112 | 1:10 3/5 | 1:23 2/5 | 1:36 1/5 | 1:50 4/5 |
| $35,000 | 108 | 1:11 | 1:23 4/5 | 1:36 3/5 | 1:51 1/5 |
| $25,000 | 104 | 1:11 1/5 | 1:24 1/5 | 1:37 | 1:52 4/5 |
| $20,000 | 100 | 1:11 3/5 | 1:24 3/5 | 1:37 3/5 | 1:52 1/5 |
| $15,000 | 96 | 1:11 4/5 | 1:24 4/5 | 1:37 4/5 | 1:52 3/5 |
| $12,500 | 92 | 1:12 1/5 | 1:25 1/5 | 1:38 1/5 | 1:53 |
| $10,000 | 88 | 1:12 2/5 | 1:25 2/5 | 1:38 3/5 | 1:53 2/5 |

racing program with each track record and then averaging the net difference.

(The track record is assigned 100 points. Each 1/5th second is worth one point. Thus a speed rating of 92 means the horse ran 1-3/5 seconds — 8/5ths, or 8 points — slower than the track record, a very good clocking. If the average of all races run that day was indeed 1-3/5 seconds seconds slower than the respective track records, the Daily Racing Form track variant would be listed as 08 in the p.p's).

But consider this: The Daily Racing Form track variant doesn't give us a clue if the 08 variant was the result of ordinary horses running on a fast track or fast horses running on an ordinary track. And this: On a day when the variant is 25 (five seconds slow) or larger, the Daily Racing Form variant is supposedly telling us the track was slow. But, realistically, we can not conclude anything about the speed of the track without knowing if slow or fast horses were involved in the day's races. This is precisely why class par research and parallel time charts pay dividends to speed figure handicappers.

The parallel time chart we have been using for this discussion shows class par clockings for 6 furlongs, 7 furlongs, one mile and 1⅛ miles. Consider the relative speed at different class levels. Consider the mathematical certainty that a horse loses some speed the farther it travels. A good parallel time chart will allow for the loss of speed over longer distances. It also shows that the classier the horse, the faster it will run.

In the sample chart, a speed figure of 116 equals 1:10-2/5 at 6 furlongs, which in turn equals 1:23 at 7 furlongs. At one mile, 116 equals 1:35-4/5. At 1⅛ miles, 116 equals 1:50-1/5, which takes into account the extra turn at 1⅛ miles.

The mathematics of racing may leave most of us cold, but there are some hidden jewels about handicapping to be gleaned from all this research. Let's take one more look at Secretariat's incredible 31-length victory in the 1973 Belmont Stakes. We may learn something about how *pace makes the race.*

Secretariat earned an astronomical 141 speed figure that day, running 1½ miles in 2:24 flat. At the 6-furlong pole, he was in a head-to-head duel with Sham and the clock said 1:09 4/5, a blistering pace that would have won 80 percent of all New York sprint stakes that year. If the finish line had been at 6 furlongs, Secretariat would have earned an excellent 124 speed figure. The final figure of 141 was earned because Secretariat *continued to race at a speed that defies the parallel time chart.*

To earn a 124 speed figure for 1½ miles, Secretariat only would have needed to finish the race in 2:25-4/5. Instead, he held his speed and finished the race at a faster rate than expected. To appreciate how remarkable his display of speed was, we only need to recall what happened to Sham, the horse that was dueling Secretariat through the early stages.

Sham, a good horse in its own right, had been second to Secretariat in the Kentucky Derby and Preakness. After dueling with Secretariat in the Belmont during the first 6 furlongs, Sham drifted to last, 46 lengths behind the champion. He simply could not keep pace.

# Understanding odds and the tote board

The head bone's connected to the neck bone, the neck bone's connected to the backbone, the backbone's connected to the hipbone — even at the racetrack. Consider **the pari-mutuel betting system.**

With each dollar wagered at most tracks, including Canterbury Downs, the track and state take approximately 20 percent off the top. This 20 percent is subdivided into the track's share, the state's share and a share designated for purses.

Each respective share filters down to several subcategories, all of which are important to a healthy racing scene.

Using 1985 betting-handle estimates, the Canterbury purse fund for 1985 has been set at $1.23 million for stakes and approximately $5.5 million for all other races. The state share, expected to be $5.8 million in 1985, will be used to equip the drug-testing lab, to pay salaries for stewards and state veterinarians and for administrative costs. The track's share, about $12 million, has been earmarked for staff salaries, bank loans, construction and maintenance costs.

A day at the track is designed to be fun, with a sporting chance to win some money. But if the player doesn't understand the pari-mutuel system, the experience may cost more than it should.

Here are some fundamental realities to consider:

■ Every bet affects the odds on every horse in the race, although it takes many small bets to equal the effect of one large wager.

■ **The tote board** in the infield shows the total amount of money bet on all horses in the win, place, and show betting pools. Only the approximate win odds are displayed on this board, along with daily double and exacta payoff possibilities. Approximate place and show payoffs can be computed by an astute player, but before we introduce how to do that, let's first examine the way the win pool works.

A **morning line** is posted at the start of a fresh betting cycle. This is an early estimate of probable odds by a track employee. Theoretically, it combines two ideas — an estimate of each horse's chance to win the race and the way the linemaker expects the crowd to perceive those chances.

The morning line at Canterbury Downs is going to be difficult to construct but interesting to watch. This region never has had pari-mutuel thoroughbred racing. The majority of patrons will be learning the game during the season.

After a few minutes of actual betting, the morning line will be replaced by actual odds. These odds are updated every 30 to 40 seconds, until betting is shut off at the official post time. These odds are not payoff odds. They merely reflect the flow of betting dollars. Payoff odds are final odds, after betting is terminated.

Once the betting begins, the pari-mutuel system continuously recomputes all wagers, totaling them, deducting the 20 percent takeout, assigning approximate win odds according to the ratio of money bet on each horse. No bet is allowed into the system after the machines lock at post time.

Suppose you're at Canterbury and you like the No. 10 horse to win the next race. One minute after the betting cycle begins, you look up at the tote board and see that No. 10 is listed at **3-5** odds. You decide to bet $2 on No. 10, which goes on to win the race one-half hour later, paying **$3.20.**

This is how the payoff would have been computed by the pari-mutuel system: After one minute of betting, we will say the win pool shows $800, including $400 to win on No. 10. The approximate win odds for each horse will be similarly displayed on the tote board and on TV monitors throughout the track. In this instance, No. 10's odds will be 3-5, which translates to 60 cents profit for each $1 wagered.

But wait a minute. These early odds are not payoff odds. Actual payoffs are calculated only after the betting period is over — at post time — when closing odds are *posted* on the tote board.

This is why early betting sometimes is a mistake. Although track management tends to encourage early betting to keep the flow going smoothly and though on busy days there is a danger of being shut out, good players wait until the middle of a betting cycle, or later, for more reliable odds information.

For the purpose of this illustration, we will assume that No. 10 has been bet at the same 3-5 odds ratio right up to post time, with a total pool of $80,000, including $40,000 on No. 10. That's why our $2 win ticket paid $3.20, or 60 cents profit for every dollar invested.

The pari-mutuel system calculated the payoff as follows: The computer deducted $16,000 (20 percent) from the $80,000, leaving a balance of $64,000 in the win pool. This $64,000 included $40,000 bet on No. 10. When our horse won the race, we shared in the $24,000 that was left in the pool by losing players. This $24,000 represents the profit created in this situation only.

If another horse had won the race, say at 12-1 odds, the $40,000 bet on No. 10 would have been lost by his supporters and become part of the profit pool.

In the case of No. 10, the computer calculated the win payoff odds by comparing the $24,000 profit in the pool to $40,000 bet on the winner. The computer next reduced this ratio to $2.40 to $4 and sliced it in half to $1.20 to $2, which equaled a $3.20 win payoff.

A $20 win bet on No. 10 would have returned $32 at the cashier's window. A $15 bet would have paid $24.

At Canterbury Downs, the Auto-Tote pari-mutuel system will be used, which is designed for betting and cashing at the same windows.

# Place and show betting do have possibilities

The pari-mutuel betting system simultaneously computes many different forms of wagers, transmitting payoff possibilities for exactas, daily doubles and other exotic wagers to TV monitors throughout the grandstand and clubhouse.

At the start of the inaugural meet at Canterbury Downs, a $2 minimum wager will be used for win, place, show, daily doubles and exacta betting; a $2 Pick Six is tentatively scheduled to be introduced in mid-season.

As we continue to explore the mechanics of racetrack betting, we should keep these things in mind:

■ The pari-mutuel system computes place and show payoffs in the same manner as win payoffs, but with a crucial difference.

Prior to the race, the odds on a given horse to place and/or show are not displayed, not measured in fixed ratios such as 12-1, or 3-5, et cetera. Place and show payoff possibilities vary according to which horses finish 1-2 or 1-2-3. It is not possible to know the exact payoff until *after* the race is run.

■ The win pool is separate from the place pool, which is separate from the show pool.

To bet "to place" does *not* require that the horse has to finish second. Nor does "show" mean a third-place finish ... To cash a place bet, the horse must finish *second or better*. To cash a show bet, the horse must finish *third or better*. An example of place payoffs appears below. There are eight horses in this hypothetical race, with $60,000 in total place bets.

# How to read the tote board

Final time
of winning horse

Time of day

Actual odds
based on wagering*

| TRACK | 4· | | TIME·DAY | TOTAL ODDS | 1  17 | 2  3 | 3  14 | 4  30 | 5  20 |
|---|---|---|---|---|---|---|---|---|---|
| FAST | M 3· | | 4·34 | 501079 WIN | 22836 | 00483 | 26694 | 12624 | 5531 |
| | E 2· | | 8THRACE | 179124 PLACE | 12313 | 25641 | 11207 | 7115 | 3156 |
| | R 1· | | POST 4·36 | 86299 SHOW | 6589 | 10600 | 5463 | 5215 | 3115 |

Condition
of track

Fractional times
of leading horse
at each quarter mile

Approximate
starting time
of race

Number of race

Amounts wagered to win, place
and show on all horses in race*

*Totals of amounts wagered and actual odds will change as betting progresses.

| | |
|---|---|
| **No. 1** | $4,000 |
| **No. 2** | $8,500 |
| **No. 3** | $12,000 |
| **No. 4** | $9,000 |
| **No. 5** | $10,000 |
| **No. 6** | $5,500 |
| **No. 7** | $10,000 |
| **No. 8** | $1,000 |

If the official finish is 1-3 or 3-1, No. 1 would pay $10 to place; No. 3 would pay $4.60 to place.

The computer figured the payoffs by first deducting the 20 percent takeout off the top ($12,000), leaving a net pool of $48,000. Next, the amount bet on No. 1 and No. 3 was combined ($4,000 and $12,000, respectively). This $16,000 total was then subtracted from the $48,000 net pool, leaving a profit of $32,000. The profit pool was split in half, assigning $16,000 to No. 1 place bettors and $16,000 to those that bet No. 3 to place. (Show payoffs are figured exactly the same as place payoffs, except there are three winning groups of ticket holders to be considered at all levels of the calculations.)

In the place payoff situation, the odds on No. 1 were $16,000 (profit) to $4,000 (invested), or 4-1, which equaled a $10 payoff for every $2 bet. The payoff was $10, not $8, because the original $2 bet was not part of the profit pool. The $10 payoff includes $8 in profit along with the original $2 bet.

By following this identical procedure, the odds on the No. 3 horse would figure to be $16,000 to $12,000, or approximately $1.30 to $1, for a payoff of $4.60. In the strictest sense, the odds are actually 1.33 to 1, but in the United States, all pari-mutuel payoffs are rounded off to the nearest, lowest dime. Thus $1.33 to $1 becomes $1.30 to $1. The bettor never sees the extra three cents per dollar. This is called *breakage* and it is very important to many people, including the frequently overlooked racing fan.

110

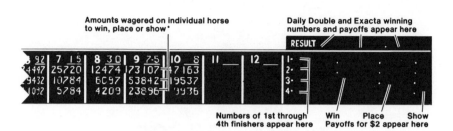

At most tracks, the breakage becomes the property of the state, the track, the purse fund, or some combination of all three. Although seemingly an insignificant sum, a few pennies of breakage may mean the difference between a payoff of $2.80 or $3, a difference that raises the pari-mutuel takeout almost 10 percent. This is one reason why it takes great skill and tremendous patience to make a profit consistently betting odds-on favorites to place and show. They finish in the money approximately 75 percent of the time, but in all but a few cases, the taxes on them are significantly higher and the payoffs are lower than they should be.

Nevertheless, place and show betting does have its possibilities. There are some occasions when the rewards are greater than the mathematical odds.

Several times a season, a show payoff may turn out to be *larger* than the place (or win) payoff on the same horse. That's because each pool is separate from each other. The money bet in one pool never affects the payoff odds in the other pools.

I've seen it many times: A top horse is bet heavily to win and ignored in the place, or show pool. Or perhaps the reverse is true . . . The crowd bets an inordinate amount of money on a steady sort to place and show, leaving his win odds at an inflated price. In any single week at any racetrack in the country, there are generous place and show payoffs caused by overzealous bettors. At Canterbury Downs this summer, we are likely to see every variety of payoff possibility, including some that rarely occur. A player could do worse than learn how to spot generous place and show payoffs.

# Solid tips for winning picks

When there are nine race cards at Canterbury Downs, there will be 31 different wagering pools, including a daily double on the first two races, three exactas scattered throughout the card and the usual win, place and show pools on every race.

On 10 race cards, there will be 35 betting opportunities, including an added exacta. That's a lot of wagering choices to consider, even for experienced players. Preparation is the key.

If possible, do some preliminary handicapping before arriving at the track.

The advance edition of the Daily Racing Form, which will be sold at Canterbury Downs and select newsstands throughout the Twin Cities, will include past performances for *tomorrow's* races. The Star and Tribune also will provide a wide range of useful information, including comprehensive result charts from the previous day's races and handicapping for that day's racing card.

Result charts give an informed player a significant edge in determining if a jockey or trainer suddenly has turned hot or or cold or if track conditions are favorable to front-running or stretch-running types. Whenever such a track bias becomes dominant, no race can be successfully handicapped without taking it into account.

The Star and Tribune's handicapping format will offer selections and comments about the races to be run, along with handicapping hints. A good player will use such information as a guide to his own selections, not as a touting service. Selections are made a day in advance, without scratches, jockey changes, or changes in track conditions. These changes are extremely important and will be available in the official track program and through the public address system at the track.

A good player knows to hold off on his final selections until he has factored in this late information. And a good player does not blindly bet someone else's selections; he learns to trust his own judgment.

Racing is a game that rewards the rugged individualists who use common sense and penalizes the players who toss their own thinking powers to the wind.

After preliminary handicapping, the player should consider finding two or three races on the day's card in which he thinks he has spotted a live prospect for a bet. Perhaps the horse has been prepared by a leading trainer and is to be ridden by one of the better jockeys (The top 10 trainers and jockeys will be listed in the official track program).

Maybe the horse has a 20 percent or better win record or frequently shows early speed and the track has been favorable to front-runners. Or maybe he had traffic problems in his last race and still finished third.

Following is an incomplete list of past performance characteristics that might lead to a winning selection. The first few pointers are especially important in maiden races.

■ Prefer lightly raced horses to horses that have lost 12 or more races.

■ Avoid playing horses that repeatedly have finished second or third without legitimate excuses. Such horses are called *sucker horses* and the name applies to humans who insist on betting them.

■ Give credit to a horse who was second or third in its only start or is lightly raced and is meeting similar maidens today.

■ Take note of a lightly raced horse who went evenly in the middle of the pack last time out and is stretching out to a mile or more for the first time.

■ Give extra credit to any lightly raced horse who showed a sign of life in a recent race and is adding blinkers to his racing equipment. Such horses tend to show immediate improvement.

■ Expect improvement if the horse encountered traffic problems in its first or second start, or if after several starts, it showed surprising early speed last time out. Traffic trouble is a legitimate excuse for defeat. Improved early speed is a strong indicator of advancing physical condition.

■ Avoid betting on maidens who get sharply bet down from 10-1 or 12-1 to 3-1 or less in the final few minutes of wagering. Don't be a follower of the crowd; think for yourself. Ask yourself if the horse's record implies victory today or if the extra betting action is the result of a wild tip or poorly informed bettors.

■ The player should respect horses saddled by trainers who consistently win 20 percent or more of all starts.

■ Give extra credit to any horse that has won 25 percent or more of its starts.

■ Avoid playing horses dropping suspiciously in class. Horses that finished well in a $10,000 claiming race last week should *not* be entered in $5,000 claiming races this week. Similarly, a solid allowance class horse does not belong in middle- or low-grade claiming races where he can be bought cheaply. Ask yourself why the horse is being sold at a bargain price. An inappropriate drop in class may be a sign that the horse is unsound or ready to go off form.

■ Give extra credit to any horse that shows the most early speed in its racing record. Horses able to get clear of the pack at any distance in any class are always contenders, unless they are running against the grain of a stretch-runner's track bias.

■ The exception to the above rule of thumb is a horse who always gets clear of the pack but never holds on to his lead. Such horses absolutely need a front-runner's track bias or a very weak field. But even in such cases, the quitter is a bad risk unless the odds are generous.

■ If a race is loaded with early speed or is to be contested over a stretch-runner's track, consider carefully the horse with the fastest final quarter mile clocking in its most recent race. A 24-second last quarter is a very good late move, regardless of class or distance.

■ If a horse has been absent for more than 30 days, look carefully at his record to see if he ever ran well after a similar layoff. A successful trainer also would be a positive recommendation, particularly if the horse is placed today at his best racing distance or within a notch or two of his customary class.

■ If a first-time starter or out-of-town shipper gets excessively bet by the crowd, don't get sucked into the tidal wave of betting activity. Stick with your own selection or pass the race and then watch the actual result to get a line on the skill of the outfit behind the horse. If the horse wins or loses narrowly, put the trainer's name in a special place. He'll be back.

■ If any race apparently has three or more evenly matched contenders, it may be a good betting race for the track's overall mutuel handle, but it may not be the wisest race to concentrate a serious bet. This brings us back to the original point.

After preliminary handicapping, try to isolate the two or three best betting opportunities on the card for concentrated play, based on your best educated guess or handicapping judgment. This is far wiser betting strategy than playing an equal $2 or $20 per race.

There are many different ways to play this game, many different handicapping theories and betting choices. But no one ever has beaten the game while indiscriminately betting every race.

# More hints
# for handicappers

Continuing with our handicapping hints, we should realize that our stated preference for lightly raced horses extends beyond maiden races into allowance races and stakes. But it is in the maiden race where we are wise to avoid horses that repeatedly have lost races.

However, it is wrong to make ironclad rules in handicapping.

A few years ago there was a filly in New York named Madam Valentine who had lost 24 consecutive maiden races, the last dozen at one mile or longer. This was a filly who never led a race, a slow-breaking stretch-runner who rarely finished in the money. After so many poor showings, it seemed unlikely that Madam Valentine ever would win in New York.

Her trainer concurred; Madam Valentine was shipped to Atlantic City racecourse, where she promptly won a $12,500 claiming race by 15 lengths.

An appropriate drop in class can change everything. So, too, can a change in scenery and Lasix, the drug used to treat bleeders. Madame Valentine got all three at once and paid 4-1 at the Atlantic City mutuel windows.

*First-time Lasix use helps many horses return to or reach their best lifetime form.* The drug not only curbs bleeding in the nasal passages but allows for easier breathing. Informal studies at several northeastern racetracks have shown that first-time Lasix horses win about 22 percent of all starts, regardless of odds or past performance characteristics, a statistic worth remembering.

Here are more handicapping hints to file away. The first two refer to allowance races for nonwinners of a race other than maiden or claiming.

■ Give strong preference to stakes-placed horses who have not lost several races in similar allowance company.

■ Give extra credit to a multiple claiming race winner over persistent allowance race losers and/or a recent maiden graduate, unless the maiden graduate won his race in superior time at a comparable distance. Successful claiming horses have one major characteristic that recent maiden graduates do not possess. *They have defeated winners.*

In races beyond a mile, (called *routes*, or *route races)*, horses with proven distance ability deserve solid preference over horses stretching out in distance. Nevertheless, one should have a knowledge of breeding, trainers and track bias before feeling confident about such selections.

■ Horses bred to run best at one mile or more may show sudden improvement when stretched out in distance.

■ Horses trained by distance specialists similarly may be ready for a new career at longer distances. Players who keep notes on trainers will have a big edge on those who do not.

■ Horses with an even turn of speed are excellent prospects to carry their speed beyond a mile, while sprinters who exhibit a good stretch kick may well lose their best punch when stretched out to a mile or more. Again, knowledge of track bias, breeding and trainers can be extremely important in anticipating such tendencies.

When thinking about routes vs. sprints, keep in mind that the pace of a 6-furlong sprint usually is *faster* than the first 6 furlongs of a race beyond a mile. This has two clear-cut effects on horses shifting from one distance to another.

■ Sprinters stretching out in distance will be *closer* to the lead in slower-paced route races.

■ Routers, who are accustomed to a slower pace found in the longer races, frequently drift farther back off the early pace in sprints.

■ A router who races with or near the leaders in a route race usually gains stamina not otherwise obtainable. Often, this added stamina reflects itself in a much improved stretch-running performance at the shorter sprint distances. Such horses changing their distance from a route to a sprint are said to be *turning back in distance.*

■ A horse turning back in distance who has shown no early speed in recent route races is *not likely* to be a factor in sprints. If such a horse lacks early speed in slower-paced routes, he hardly can be expected to keep pace in a faster sprint race.

In all races, the player's objective should be to find contenders that have been well prepared for the task at hand. Good recent races or signs of improvement are a must. Such signs would include newly developed speed, an appropriate drop in class, the addition of Lasix, or blinkers, or perhaps a logical switch in distance. These signs of improvement often are reinforced by the four most recent workouts published beneath the past performance profile.

■ A positive hint for improvement might include at least one workout of any kind since last week's race. When a horse works between starts, he generally is fit enough to hold his form or improve upon it.

■ Two works since a race 14 days ago similarly is a positive sign of conditioning and if the horse is attempting a longer distance today, it is comforting to find a workout pattern designed to stretch the horse out.

■ A series of three or four workouts that complement two or three races stretching back over 20-30 days. Such a pattern of activity rarely is maintained by a poorly conditioned horse.

■ A series of workouts in which the most recent work or works are faster than prior works. When a horse improves in his workouts, his races usually follow suit.

The best use of this or any other handicapping list would be to add your own valid insights. When preparing for a day at Canterbury, make your own selections. The racing game is more fun for those who think logically for themselves and hardly profitable for those who blindly follow tips or the opinions of the crowd.

# The right horse
# in the right race

A friend of mine tells this tale about the two biggest bets he ever made. My friend is a $2 player who occasionally bets $10 or $20 on horses he likes a whole lot.

"I was at Bowie racetrack in Maryland during the 1970s on a day when the track was frozen and every race was won by the horse who took the lead right out of the starting gate. The rail was like an interstate highway and the rest of the track was like a plowed field.

"Every year the track would get like that for a few days in the dead of winter and I finally caught on."

My friend was proud of his observation and he did well throughout the winter meet by paying careful attention to which horses raced on the favored rail path and which ones had been forced to run through the slower footing.

In mid-January, he cashed a longshot daily double by betting a single $10 ticket on the No. 1 horse in the first race with the No. 1 in the second race, the only two front-running horses in either contest. The winning ticket was worth $385.

In mid-February, my friend was headed for his first winning season at Bowie, ahead nearly $1,000 without ever having bet more than $40 in a single race.

Then came a horse named Right Judex.

Right Judex was a $5,000 claiming horse, a 3-year-old Maryland-bred entered in a 1 and 1/16th-mile race for $5,000 claiming horses bred in Maryland. Such restricted races tend to be inflated in value. Horses who run in open, nonrestricted races generally are superior to state-bred horses of similar claiming value.

Right Judex had the rail and the most early speed. My friend bet $80 on him . . . and lost. Right Judex finished second, a loser because his apprentice jockey, Danny Wright, gunned him to the lead and kept on driving all the way around the track. Right Judex tired and drifted wide turning for home, losing the rail and the advantage.

The following week, Right Judex was entered in a Maryland-bred stakes race, an apparently impossible spot for a $5,000 claiming horse, especially one who had lost his last race despite having the favorable inside post.

The favorite for this stakes was Bee Bee Bee, just up from Florida, where he had finished a respectable fourth in the Flamingo Stakes. But Right Judex had the rail on a frozen track and this time Danny Wright didn't waste the opportunity.

My friend didn't bet on him. "Bee Bee Bee has too much class," he explained before passing on the race. But after the race — after watching Right Judex beat Bee Bee Bee by 14 lengths — my friend could only shake his head.

Seven weeks later, at Pimlico racetrack, the prestigious Preakness stakes was being run. Riva Ridge, the Kentucky Derby winner, was the 1-5 favorite; No Le Hace, second in the Derby, was the 7-2 second choice, and Key to the Mint, on the comeback trail, was the third choice at 9-2 odds.

It was pouring rain. The track was under water and Riva Ridge was a dead duck, a colt who had turned in the two worst races of his life on wet tracks, a probable loser who, because of his TV exposure in the Kentucky Derby, was being seriously overbet by the 40,000 in attendance.

No Le Hace was a distinct threat to upset, but because of the extremely sloppy track, all races that day had been won by front-running speed horses. No Le Hace was a confirmed stretch runner.

Key to the Mint was similarly in a tough spot to upset. A future champion, he was tackling a seasoned group and had only a single race at one mile in his recent past performances and he, too, had a stretch-runner's profile.

The eventual winner of this Preakness was, believe it or not, Bee Bee Bee, who paid $39.40. Very few handicappers had given him a tumble.

After the race, I saw my friend bouncing his way through the grandstand crowd on his way out the door, smiling from ear to ear. Early next morning, I called him to ask what happened.

"I bet $40 to win and $40 to place on Bee Bee Bee,' he said.

"How could you have possibly done that," I asked, reminding him that Bee Bee Bee had been slaughtered by Right Judex only two months before.

"Easy," he replied with the satisfaction of a man who knew he had made a brilliant selection.

"Just because he lost to a cheap horse on a biased track didn't bother me. Yesterday, he was the only speed in the field and the only horse who ever won a race in the mud."

Sometimes, the obvious winner is *not* the best horse in the race, but the right horse in the right race, at the right time. Bee Bee Bee never won another race in his life, while three weeks later, on a dry track, Riva Ridge went on to score a convincing win in the Belmont Stakes. As for my friend, he still is a $2 bettor who occasionally steps up his action to suit his enthusiasm, but he has a commissioned painting of Bee Bee Bee on his living room wall.

# Practical advice
# on betting strategies

There is considerable entertainment value in selecting a horse for any reason and then betting it to win, place or show. But if a player wants to improve his chances of success, he will need a sensible betting strategy.

Betting strategies take as many different forms as handicapping methods. Some people like to bet equal amounts on every race, some like to concentrate their play on one, two or three races. It's a matter of style, bankroll and experience.

Newcomers to the sport might consider the following ideas and suggestions. A good betting strategy does not have to be sophisticated or complicated, but it can save the player money as well as promote his or her chances for success.

■ Before figuring how much to bring to the track for betting purposes, a player would be well-advised to consider his bankroll already spent as entertainment. A popular slogan dealing with the dangers of gambling excesses should be kept in mind: Bet with your head, not over it.

■ Good players prepare for a day's races with advance handicapping and concentrate their play on one, two or three best bets. Some refrain from playing any other races, but most are willing to risk a few dollars on scattered plays throughout the day.

■ The criteria for a concentrated wager, called a **prime bet**, varies from player to player but obviously reflects the player's confidence in his selection.

■ Playing the daily double — which requires picking the winner of both the first and second races on the same ticket — increases the player's odds against cashing a winning ticket, but the payoffs are correspondingly larger. When a player prefers one horse for a possible prime bet in either the first or the second race, he presses his luck in the daily double if he fails to reserve a portion of his wager for a straight win bet.

Here are a few typical daily double plays, including one that shows when a compatible win bet would also make good sense.

(a) A $2 crisscross involving two horses in the first race with two horses in the second would work out to be an $8 bet.

(b) A $2 crisscross involving three horses in each daily double race would involve nine combinations at a cost of $18.

(c) Three horses in the first race with two horses in the second would cost $12. Four horses in the first with two horses in the second would cost $16 at the $2 basic unit of play. If a player likes one of the horses in the race a little more than the rest, he could consider playing one extra $2 ticket on all the tickets involving the preferred key horse.

For example: A $4 double on Nos. 1, 2 and 3 with No. 1 and $2 doubles on Nos. 1, 2 and 3 with No. 2 in the second race would cost $12, (three tickets at $4 apiece), plus $6 (three tickets at $2 apiece), for a total of $18. If one of the $4 double combination turns out to be the winning combination, the player would cash a pair of $2 winning double tickets.

(d) When playing one horse as a **key** selection in a daily double with two, three or more horses in the second race (or vise versa), it is wise to reserve a sizable percentage of the intended wager for a straight win bet on the key horse. This is a very important point to remember and the following is an example of this betting strategy:

Assume the player likes one horse (a key horse) in the first race with four contenders in the second. A $2 daily double play would cost $8 to tie up the four combinations. But in this instance, the player would be making a mistake if he failed to bet a similar amount on his preferred selection to win. The total wager involving the key horse should be $16, which would include an $8 win bet on the key horse in addition to the $8 played in the doubles. If $16 is too steep, the player should not lower his win bet but forget the daily double instead.

The $8 bet on the double and $8 in the win pool reflects a sound 50-50 balance to keep in mind, regardless of the unit of wager.

The bottom line for a good betting strategy is this: Daily doubles and exactas offer profit-boosting opportunities because the payoffs are larger than straight win prices. But the worst mistake a player can make is to correctly select a winner and not earn a dime.

Consider how frustrating it is to pick a winner and watch the payoff prices go up on the tote board while you are tearing up parimutuel tickets on the daily double.

Racing is a game that tests the mind as well as provides plenty of entertainment and fun. But when a player is handicapping properly, he should cash in on his insight and not be seduced by visions of enormous payoffs. Daily doubles and exactas are excellent bets, providing the player does not concentrate all his play on them.

Place and show betting likewise offers conservative players a vehicle to participate on a modest scale. Some players prefer to bet huge sums of money on heavy favorites to place or show. But the bottom line for a sensible betting strategy is to favor win betting above all other forms of wagering.

# The racing fan needs accurate information

During one week in the spring, I visited Hialeah Park in Miami, the Fair Grounds racetrack in New Orleans, Garden State Park in Cherry Hill, N.J., and Santa Anita Park in Arcadia, Calif.

A traveling fan is bound to find many differences between racetracks, especially in the way he is treated by track management.

This was seen clearly at the four racetracks I visited. Three of the four have serious management problems. Strangely enough, one of those three is Garden State Park, which opened in March.

Garden State's problems have nothing to do with the track itself, or perhaps with the new management team, headed by banker-breeder Robert Brennan. The problem stems from Keystone racetrack, the nearby Philadelphia facility that filled the void when Garden State burned in 1977. Ever since Keystone opened in 1974, its track management has ignored fan complaints about inaccurate workout times and other pertinent handicapping information. Keystone also is poorly ventilated and lacks creature comforts.

The bottom line — fan attendance — has spoken volumes about the way Delaware Valley racing fans disapprove of Keystone's policies. Keystone never has handled more than half of the attendance or betting handle of the old Garden State. This explains why Brennan and his associates bought Keystone six months after they began construction on the new Garden State. It also explains why Brennan has set a course to reaffirm Garden State's position as a first-class racetrack. Nothing less than that will overcome the insensitive treatment people in his market have known for the past decade.

The Fair Grounds racetrack also has failed to treat its customers to accurate handicapping information, although the 113-year-old facility retains its charm and fits nicely with the tempo of the French Quarter.

The $3 minimum wager is another sore spot with racing fans. In my visit to the Fair Grounds on Louisiana Derby Day, several fans said they believed the minimum $3 wager reflected management's desire to get as much money out of them as possible. With that kind of response to a rather dubious experiment, one would think management would revert to the familiar $2 minimum unit, but that hasn't happened.

The betting handle and daily attendance figures have dropped 10 percent since the $3 wager was introduced two years ago.

Hialeah Park also has serious problems, although the track would not be operating today if John Brunetti had not rescued it nearly a decade ago. Hialeah is located next to a high-crime area and most veteran residents of south Florida have migrated 20 to 30 miles to the north, nearer to Gulfstream Park. Gulfstream has capitalized on this growth with a forward-thinking program of improvements, forcing the Florida's Division of Pari-Mutuel Wagering to give Gulfstream the premier winter dates on the annual racing calendar.

The Flamingos still fly at Hialeah and the racing surface still is one of the safest in the nation, but Brunetti is fighting a battle of survival with his track. Costs have been cut in many key areas. The success or failure of Brunetti's management depends not upon his efforts, but on the Florida Highway Department and the Florida Legislature. Unless Florida builds a modern highway connecting Hialeah with the new population center in the region, the morale at the track will continue to slip as will the attendance and handle. And until the Legislature lower its share of the pari-mutuel handle, Brunetti will be unable to increase stagnant purses that further threaten the overall appeal of this once elegant horse park.

Santa Anita Park is by far the classiest, most successful track of the four. It may be the best run racing park in the United States.

Impressively nestled in the foothills of the San Gabriel Mountains, Santa Anita offers top-quality racing, a beautifully maintained physical plant, near-gourmet quality food and a carefully designed infield that features several playgrounds and picnic areas. More importantly, Santa Anita goes out of its way to provide fans with a regular flow of accurate handicapping information.

Workouts are properly identified and accurately timed from picturesque Clocker's Corner, with the public invited for breakfast. Horseshoe information — not available at Garden State Park nor at the Fair Grounds — are publicly announced at Santa Anita (At Hialeah, the information is available, but only with a trip to the paddock area).

Santa Anita management also seems to recognize the need for detailed statistics on jockeys and trainers in its track program, although there is room for improvement in its disclosure policy about drugs for racing purposes.

After years of failing to reveal which horses are being treated with Bute and/or Lasix, Santa Anita decided to publicly display such information at scattered locations around the track grounds. Trainers are permitted to bet on their horses and if they know which horse is being treated with what drug, so should everyone else.

Santa Anita averages 32,000 fans per day who bet an average of $5.5 million on each nine-race card.

Although Minnesota's first racetrack is not likely to approach half those figures, the Santa Anita management team that has been behind the Minnesota racing experiment promises the same enlightened policies to be in force at Canterbury. Judging by the way they run Santa Anita, there is no reason to expect we will not get it.

# Laffit Pincay Jr., world's best jockey

Laffit Pincay's expert ride aboard Skywalker in the Santa Anita Derby last April perfectly illustrates the importance of the jockey in thoroughbred racing.

Few jockeys win with horses that are unfit or overmatched. But every track has several riders who lose races they should win, complemented by others who dominate the results.

In New York, Angel Cordero Jr., Jorge Velasquez and a few other stars fit this winning mold. In Louisiana, Randy Romero is head and shoulders above the rest and at Oaklawn Park in Arkansas, the same can be said for Patrick Day.

At Santa Anita Park, where the purses are the biggest in the game, there are 10 to 15 outstanding jockeys, including national money champion Chris McCarron, two-time Kentucky Derby winner Eddie Delahoussaye and newcomer Gary Stevens. Hall of Famer William Shoemaker also rides there. But despite their credentials, none matches Laffit Pincay Jr., who is simply the world's best jockey.

Pincay's special skills include all the fundamentals necessary to be a great jockey: strength in his legs and hands, patience in traffic, knowledge of pace and a solid whip technique. But, above all, the secret to Pincay's success is his extraordinary *timing*.

Many times a season, Pincay will do what he did with Skywalker in the Santa Anita Derby — bringing a seemingly defeated horse back into contention late in the race. That's because Pincay is a master at waiting until the last possible second before he goes to an all-out drive. Like McCarron and Shoemaker, Pincay doesn't rush his horses; he *sits chilly,* keeping them as calm as possible. But unlike McCarron and Shoemaker, Pincay doesn't rely on finesse in the stretch drive. Pincay is a pure power rider.

He rides as if he were driving a sports car, maintaining his balance on the turns, changing gears smoothly, applying the strongest finishing technique the game has ever seen.

Where tough-minded Cordero might appear to be a man of constant motion, Pincay is noticeably relaxed. Where Shoemaker appears to ride with his wrists, relying on his sensitive hands, Pincay's muscular forearms always seem perfectly rigid, maintaining absolute control over the horse regardless of his position in the race.

Pincay at his best is Pincay guiding his horse to a good position, stalking the pace, waiting for an opening, moving between horses, angling to the inside coming off the final turn, uncorking his whip in deep stretch.

Where Velasquez — himself a terrific finisher — might pull out all the stops turning for home, Pincay is far more likely to wait until the final eighth mile before bringing his whip into play. It was this patient application of the whip that helped Skywalker win the Santa Anita Derby and it has worked for Pincay in many other stakes.

With the finish line in sight, Pincay is always in synch with his horse, uncorking his whip, snapping it on the right or left flank, shaking it under the horse's eyes, judging the response and switching to the other flank if necessary, without missing a beat.

Three or four strides from the wire, Pincay almost always packs the whip away, lowers his body to minimize wind resistance, extends his pumping arms forward through to the finish, giving his horse every chance to win the photo.

Watching Pincay rise out of the saddle, easing his mount to a gallop, turning him around quietly for the canter back to the winner's circle is like watching a polished equestrian who has just won the gold medal at the Olympics. The man is more than poetry in motion, he is a gifted, exceedingly strong athlete, a living textbook on horsemanship, a man who competes without fear in a tough, exceedingly dangerous sport.

The next time you see Laffit Pincay Jr. ride in a televised race or in person, even if he is aboard a probable loser, watch him closely. Win or lose, you just might be looking at the best jockey who ever lived.

# An exacta betting system for novices

George Wilson is 48, a successful radio executive in southern California. He is an ex-minor league baseball player, a happily married man with seven children, including two preschoolers. George also is a horseplayer, a very good one. In early April at Santa Anita, he won several hundred dollars in three days by playing a wonderful betting system.

Wilson, a typical racing fan, has a big heart. He is willing to share his system, free of charge, as his contribution to the Minnesota racing experiment. "There's no reason why newcomers to the sport shouldn't have a good time," he said.

Wilson's system does not require hours of study, it doesn't keep him awake at night analyzing past performance records. He doesn't keep track of jockey's and trainer's records, doesn't watch races like a hawk, doesn't observe the horses in the prerace warmups. Wilson doesn't even buy the Daily Racing Form.

"I do buy a track program though," he explained. "I also buy a few local newspapers and one of the tout sheets sold at the track. I like to see who the experts are picking; it helps me later when I put my betting system to work."

Wilson's betting system concentrates on exactas and daily doubles, which are the primary exotic wagering devices that will be available at Canterbury Downs. Wilson rarely bets to win, tailoring his game to match his personality.

"That's very important," he said. "I know I'm a lousy handicapper, but I have a good feel for odds and betting strategies. I also learned a long time ago not to press, not to chase after losses if the system isn't working and there will be times when it won't. But the secret to this game is very straightforward. No matter what method of handicapping you use, no matter what betting technique, the secret is to keep your betting small until you have begun to win. That's the time to get aggressive, not before."

Here is Wilson's system for betting exactas. He says not to expect miracles but that it has worked for him for more than 15 years. It is simple to employ and is ideal for novice players.

**Step 1/** Check the official track program for the morning-line odds and note the longest shot listed. For example, in the ninth race April 7 at Santa Anita, the longest shot was No. 4, Proud Thief, at 15-1. As explained before, the morning line is constructed by a professional handicapper employed by the track. The morning line is only a guide; the actual odds change regularly through the betting cycle, with the final payoffs based on post-time odds.

**Step 2/** Check the exacta payoff possibilities linking each horse with all the other horses in the race. These payoffs are displayed in sequence during the betting cycle on television monitors throughout the track. The display will list all the different exacta payoffs involving No. 1 to win with Nos. 2, 3, 4, 5, 6, 7 or 8 finishing second. The payoffs involving No. 2 will similarly be displayed on the monitor, followed by the payoffs involving No. 3, etc. In this case, we are interested in the payoffs involving No. 4 to win, with 1, 2, 3, 5, 6, 7, 8 to finish second.

**Step 3/** When the payoffs for No. 4 are displayed, note which three horses offer the *lowest* exacta payoffs. Wilson's system calls for a three-horse box on these horses. This is a bet involving six different combinations. If any two of the three numbers finish 1-2, the exacta bet will be won. If only one of the three horses finishes first, or second, the exacta bet will be lost. At Santa Anita, where there is a $5 minimum exacta bet, the cost for this three-horse box was $30. At Canterbury, where the minimum exacta wager will be $2, the same three-horse box will cost $12.

In the SAnta Anita example, the three lowest exacta payoffs with No. 4 to win were Nos. 2, 3 and 8, despite the fact No. 8 wound up going to the post as only the sixth choice in the win pool, at 8-1 odds. Wilson's system had detected a *live* horse in the exacta pool, a horse getting more play than usual, and the final race result turned out to be No. 3 finishing first and No. 8 second for a $294.50 payoff. If this exacta had been run at Canterbury, the 3-8 combination would have paid $117.80 for $2.

Wilson explains the reason why he uses the *longest* shot in the morning line as a key to determine his play.

"I handicapped races for 10 years but never could win, until I began to pay attention to betting patterns in exactas and daily doubles," he said. "I found that informed players or trainers like to wheel solid horses with everything in the race. This kind of concentrated action on a single horse didn't always show up in the win, place or show pools. It's too obvious there. But the action on these live horses often showed up in the exacta payoffs — you could see it knock the price down on every exacta possibility, especially with the longest shot in the race."

Wilson's system is based on a fine piece of betting logic, a logic that says few people bet serious money on hopeless longshots. But they may bet more money than usual in exacta combinations with every other horse in a given race, even the longest shot on the board. Wilson's system isolates extra betting action on legitimate contenders who are getting unusually heavy play.

"I figure if the horse is getting bet in the exactas with a hopeless longshot, maybe somebody knows something," Wilson says.

Perhaps so, but during Santa Anita Derby week, the somebody who knew something was decidedly George Wilson. In three days, he hit seven out of nine exactas.

# The true value
# of handicapping systems

The George Wilson betting system for exactas is one of millions of systems invented by creative horseplayers throughout the centuries. Unfortunately, the vast majority of these systems never earned their inventors a retirement villa in the Caribbean.

Most systems fail because they do not deal with the realities of racing. They pretend to reveal absolutes in a sport that defies simplistic explanations.

Nevertheless, systems do have an educational value, especially those built upon relatively sound handicapping principles. The trick is not to be seduced by systems; they rarely produce a long-term profit. Instead, it is wiser to regard a good system as a toy, a plaything, or in a more serious vein, as an opportunity to learn about handicapping through experimentation.

Perhaps one or more of the following systems will appeal to newcomers at Canterbury this summer. They are each offered with fun in mind, minus a no-risk guarantee.

## The Repeater system/

■ Check the Daily Racing Form for each horse's most recent race.

■ Eliminate all horses who did not win their most recent races.

■ If only one horse won his latest race, select him for play if that win was within 10 days of today's race; if 11 days or more, pass the race.

■ If two or more horses qualify, select the winner who won most recently. If a tie exists, pass the race.

The idea behind the repeater system is simple and effective. If a horse is good enough to win a recent race, he probably is fit enough to repeat. This system wins approximately 30 percent of the time.

## The Class Drop system/

■ Check the Daily Racing Form for each horse's most recent race.

■ Eliminate all horses who are *not* moving down in class from allowance races into a claiming race, or from a stakes race into an allowance race, or a claimer, or a maiden race.

■ If only one such horse, select him for play if he raced within 10 days of today, or if he had at least one workout listed during the past five calendar days. These workouts are published in the Daily Racing Form underneath each horse's past performance profile.

■ If two or more such dropdowns, prefer the one that has the most combined furlongs raced *and* worked out during the past 10 days.

This system says that a significant drop in class may be beneficial to the horse, but the recent racing and workout rules help eliminate totally unfit or potentially infirm horses. Dropdowns with recent racing and/or workouts are preferred to dropdowns that have been suspiciously idle.

## The top trainer-top jockey system/

■ Consult the official track program for the top 10 trainers and top 10 jockeys.

■ Rank the listed trainers and jockeys according to their win percentage, giving the top percentage trainer and jockey 10 points each; the second-ranking jockey and trainer nine points; the third eight, etc.

■ Go through the entire program and award each horse the appropriate number of points earned by having a top 10 trainer and/or jockey.

■ Pass each race where no horse has at least 10 total points.

■ If one such horse exists, it is an automatic play; if two or more have a minimum of 10 points, prefer the horse with the highest morning line odds printed in the official track program. If tied, prefer the higher point total. If still tied, play both.

This system can be a lot of fun at a strange racetrack or for novice players who do not know how to read the Racing Form.

## Longshot maiden race system/

■ Play only maiden claiming races where the price is $10,000 or less. These are races for nonwinners entered to be claimed for $10,000 or less.

■ Eliminate all horses that have raced 12 or more times in maiden claiming races or 15 times overall.

■ Eliminate all horses that have raced the last three races in maiden claiming company, regardless of claiming price.

■ If only one horse left, it is an automatic play.

■ If two or more horses, prefer the horse who raced most recently in a race with winners, or with nonclaiming maidens.

■ If no such horse, eliminate all previous starters and select the first-time starter who has worked out the most total furlongs during the past 14 days. If no such horse, pass the race.

This system picks longshots who should be given a chance to win in weak company. Low-priced maiden claimers are the slowest thoroughbreds. Frequent losers are bad risks. Horses that faced better opposition are entitled to improve at this level of competition. In a race dominated by proven losers, first-time starters do not have to be very good, just fit.

None of the above handicapping systems require in-depth knowledge of racing and yet they incorporate many sound handicapping principles. Newcomers might enjoy testing them at Canterbury. Win or lose, they will provide a lot of fun and entertainment.

# Knowledge of breeding
# is a handicapping must

In an earlier primer, we discussed the role of breeding from the standpoint of economics and inflation. We observed that stakes-winning racehorses have considerable value for stud purposes. We know that well-bred, unraced thoroughbreds may sell for millions at select yearling sales.

We specifically examined the case of Devil's Bag, who was syndicated for a record $36 million after a spectacular 2-year-old season. Even though he failed to reproduce that form at 3, we were able to forecast a probable profit for all who invested in him.

The breeding industry is a complex, multibillion dollar investment game played by small-time horse owners and giant racing-breeding farms. Shares in top sires are sold through special stock exchanges and on Wall Street. Limited partnerships are offered privately by speculators and entrepreneurs. The prospectus always includes the chance for great financial reward and tax benefits.

In Minnesota, there will be countless offerings and unique opportunities to get in on the ground floor of the state's newest industry. Some rudimentary knowledge of breeding therefore is recommended for any serious evaluation of bloodstock for racing and breeding purposes. This is equally true for handicappers, who always are asked to evaluate horses at new distances or racing surfaces.

The following pointers are fundamental to an understanding of this complex subject:

■ *Great racehorses do not always make great sires.*

Examples: Triple Crown winners Citation, Secretariat and Affirmed. All modestly successful as sires, although both Secretariat and Affirmed still are alive and may yet produce the caliber of horse everybody hopes to see from them.

■ *In evaluating a mare for a possible mating or evaluating her off-spring for the yearling sales market, her racing record is not nearly as important as her producing record. Also, if a mare never has been to stud, the producing record of her sisters may be a good clue to her own breeding potential.*

Examples: Six Crowns, dam of Chief's Crown, was a nonstakes winner, although her dam, Chris Evert, was the winner of the New York filly Triple Crown and a sister to several major stakes producers. Also, Stepping High, dam of Buckaroo, the sire of Derby winner Spend a Buck, was a $10,000 claiming filly from a good producing family.

■ *Very fast racehorses tend to produce precocious offspring.*

Examples: The get of Clever Trick, Cutlass, Danzig, Full Out, Full Pocket, Seattle Slew and Tilt Up are likely to win races early in their careers, especially at sprint distances.

■ *Some very fast horses may have breeding and racing potential beyond sprint distances.*

Examples: Alydar, a son of precociously fast Raise A Native and Seattle Slew, a grandson of Preakness winner Bold Ruler (deceased), who ranks a close second to Northern Dancer as the most prolific sire in racing history. Most sons of Northern Dancer and Bold Ruler have in turn become successful sires.

■ *Some sires pass on distinctive physical traits and racing preferences.*

Examples: Sons and grandsons of Stage Door Johnny tend to improve dramatically on grass courses and instill stamina in their offspring. There also are sires who seem to transmit the ability to handle wet racetracks.

A study by New York-based researcher Ed McNamara lists the following sires in order of their offspring's combined victories on wet New York tracks since 1983. To make the list, seven off-track victories were required. An asterisk next to a horse's name indicates a son of Bold Ruler.

Naskra, Raise A Native, Grey Dawn II, Key To The Mint, Graustark, Native Charger, Sauce Boat, Salem, Tom Rolfe, *What A Pleasure, Proudest Roman, Tri Jet, Avatar, Mr. Leader, Diplomat Way, Herberger, In Reality, *Chieftain, Icecapade, Le Fabuleaux, Little Current, *Raja Baba, Sea Bird, An Act, Blushing Groom, Cyane, Creme De La Creme, Cormorant, *Cornish Prince, Damascus, *Dewan, *King Emperor, Olden Times, Stage Door Johnny, Turn And Count.

Interestingly, all the above sires were major stakes winners and some were not noted for off-track racing ability.

Tri Jet in particular ran well below his best form on off tracks and the same was true for Riva Ridge, who needs only a few more winners to qualify for McNamara's list.

■ *The Kentucky Derby is rarely won by a horse who has weak distance breeding. Good breeding for classic racing is balanced breeding, preferably with notable speed in the sire matched to a stamina-producing dam, although the reverse typing sometimes has proven to be equally effective.*

Examples: Secretariat was by Bold Ruler out of Somethingroyal, by Princequillo. Princequillo was the leading broodmare sire of the 1960s and '70s. He also was the sire of Prince John, sire of Stage Door Johnny. Princequillo, a classic distance horse, stamped virtually all his get with extraordinary stamina.

Somethingroyal, bred by Cristopher Chenery, was one of the most prolific producers of stakes winners in racing history.

The breeding lines for this year's leading Kentucky Derby prospects are listed below, with comments according to probable distance potential.

**Chief's Crown/** By Danzig, out of Six Crowns, by Secretariat. Bred for at least one mile, possibly longer.

**Spend a Buck/** By Buckaroo out of Belle Du Jour, by Speak John. Bred for all distances.

**Proud Truth/** By Graustark out of Wake Robin, by Summer Tan. Bred for one mile and longer.

**Stephan's Odyssey/** By Danzig out of Kennelot, by Gallant Man. Bred for one mile and longer. (Gallant Man is a sire of distance horses)

**Rhoman Rule/** By Stop The Music out of Morning Bird, by Tom Fool. Bred for one mile and longer.

**Pancho Villa/** By Secretariat out of Crimson Saint, by Crimson Satan. Bred for speed, but has distance possibilities if trained for it.

**Eternal Prince/** By Majestic Prince out of Eternal Queen, by Fleet Nasrullah. Bred for speed, questionable at 1¼ miles.

# Training strategies
# for the Kentucky Derby

One of the races on the inaugural Breeders' Cup program at Hollywood Park last fall was the Breeders Cup Juvenile, contested at one mile. It was won by Chief's Crown by ½ length over Tank's Prospect, with Spend a Buck a close third. Many races later, the same three colts were among the top-rated contenders for the 111th running of the Kentucky Derby.

This despite serious injuries and illness that threatened the careers of all three horses. Chief's Crown lost two weeks of training due to a cough that killed one of his stablemates. Tank's Prospect was operated on for a problem in his windpipe after finishing last in the Santa Anita Derby. Spend a Buck had bone chips removed from his right knee over the winter.

The trainers of these three colts did textbook work bringing their horses to the threshold of the Derby at peak form.

Spend a Buck's wire-to-wire performance in the Garden State Stakes in April was an awesome display of speed, topped off by a fine finish to complete the 1⅛ mile distance in the spectacular time of 1:45-4/5. The track was very fast, but so was Spend A Buck, who finished his final eighth as quickly as he ran his first. Trainer Cam Gambolati, an obscure talent until now, did masterful work with this fast colt. His program included a 7-furlong prep stakes, a 1-mile stakes around two turns, followed by the Garden State Stakes. These three prep races were spaced two weeks apart, a pattern designed to complement the May 4 Derby.

Trainer Wayne Lukas, criticized frequently for racing his horses too often, sent Tank's Prospect to Arkansas despite throat surgery a week before and saw the colt win the richest of all Derby preps with the strongest stretch kick seen this season. Lukas, an experienced Derby trainer, vowed not to overrace Tank's Prospect before the Derby and kept his word. The colt looked very sharp at Oaklawn, vastly improved over his Breeders' Cup form.

Chief's Crown, was similarly well handled, winning both his starts, the 7-furlong Swale Stakes at Hialeah on March 2 and the 1⅛ mile Flamingo Stakes at Gulfstream on March 30. Roger Laurin's light racing and training strategy was a sign of extreme confidence in his champion colt. Before the season began, Laurin mapped out his plan for Chief's Crown and stuck to it, settling on the Blue Grass Stakes at Keeneland for the colt's final Derby prep. This strategy went against the grain of such experienced Triple Crown trainers as Woody Stephens and John Veitch.

But Laurin merely followed the path his father, Lucien, used in 1972 to train Riva Ridge. That horse won the Blue Grass and then went on to take the Kentucky Derby and the Belmont Stakes.

Veitch, trainer of Proud Truth, rejected the Blue Grass in favor of the Wood Memorial at Aqueduct "because the Blue Grass (April 25) is too close to the Derby (nine days) . . . It doesn't leave you with any time to correct for mistakes." Veitch further explained that the Wood is a superior Derby prep for another, somewhat overlooked reason. "In the Wood, all the horses carry 126 pounds. That's the weight they have to carry in the Derby."

Stephens put his No. 1 Derby threat, Stephan's Odyssey, in the Lexington Stakes at Keeneland on April 16 "because I never had any luck in the Blue Grass, it's too close to the Derby and last year I ran Swale in the Lexington."

In an interesting twist to his own logic, Stephens picked out the Derby Trial Stakes on April 27 for his second-stringer, Creme Fraiche. The Trial is contested on opening day at Churchill Downs, one week before the Derby.

"I won the Derby with Canonade (1974) using the Derby Trial and then Caveat (1983) ran a strong third off the same prep race," Stephens explained. Also," he continued, "the Trial gives a horse a race over the track, which sometimes makes a big difference."

For several years, for reasons Veitch pointed out, the most popular Kentucky Derby prep race has been the 1⅛-mile Wood Memorial, which drew a select field of six, including Proud Truth, Rhoman Rule and Eternal Prince.

"The Derby was our main objective and the Wood was only a prep," trainer Angel Penna said after Rhoman Rule put out a modest effort to finish third behind Eternal Prince and Proud Truth.

Eternal Prince's trainer, Butch Lenzini Jr., viewed the Wood differently. Although his colt cruised to a wire-to-wire win without serious pressure from any rival, Lenzini thought the race set his colt up as the horse to catch in the Derby. It didn't turn out that way, despite the fact that Lenzini, who won the 1982 Preakness with front-runner Aloma's Ruler, proved once again that he knows how to get a fast horse sharp at the right time.

Through all of these prep races we were able to watch many young horses develop, under contrasting training strategies. There were endless lessons in horsemanship to be gleaned from all of it.

# Good workouts, good form

The week before the Kentucky Derby is one of the most instructive, interesting weeks in all of sports.

Unlike the week that precedes the Super Bowl or a heavyweight championship bout, where most of the activity is designed to hype the event, Derby week is filled with important training maneuvers.

If the favorite takes a bad step in his final workout — as Sir Gaylord did in 1962 — he could be scratched or lose his edge.

If the many contenders who have survived so many races and workouts fail to maintain their training programs, or seem the least bit spent, they will surely fall by the wayside when the race is on.

Throughout Derby week, every horse will gallop 8 to 10 miles and put in at least one, perhaps two serious workouts.

These gallops, which are not timed, keep a horse fit between important works or races. They also help calm high-strung or very fast horses while building their stamina.

Whenever a horse gallops 1½ miles at a steady clip, under the snug hold of his exercise rider, he is communicating a positive message of fitness. "I'm ready," the horse is saying. "I'm fit and I want more work!"

Workouts, which are timed and published in the Daily Racing Form, can be revealing indicators of fitness. This is true for all horses, but each year the Derby horses provide us with an amazing oppportunity to learn more about the way good trainers prepare good horses. The lessons learned can be applied to other racing situations for the rest of the year.

Top-class 3-year-olds who had their final prep race two weeks before the Kentucky Derby require more work than those who performed in the Blue Grass Stakes or Derby Trial. Indeed, every Derby winner of modern times, along with most of the horses who ran well in the race, have signaled their good form by perfoming well in several prep races and by working strongly on the Churchill Downs track.

In fact, Swale, the 1984 Derby winner, overcame a lackluster final prep race with two sparkling workouts during Derby week.

Sunny's Halo, the 1983 winner, worked a sensational mile on the Sunday before the Derby, reeling off quarter-mile clockings that got faster as he went along.

Both of these Derby winners needed those demanding workouts because their final prep races were more than two weeks before the big race.

In 1982, Gato Del Sol finished second in the Blue Grass Stakes, nine days before the Derby, but tipped his hand further with a crisp 5-furlong workout in the middle of Derby week.

Pleasant Colony, the 1981 winner, came into the race with a sensational victory in the Wood Memorial and a solid 6-furlong workout eight days later.

When a trainer is cranking up a horse for a top effort, the horse must be strong enough to handle the pressure.

The workouts and gallops during Derby week help reveal which horses have reached peak form or which horses have peaked too soon.

■ A spent horse will work listlessly, or ambiguously, or not at all, leaving doubts about his fitness.

■ A short, fast work may help sharpen a horse's gate-breaking ability but will do nothing to enhance his stamina.

■ The most definitive sign to look for in a positive workout pattern is an aggressive finish. That is true for Derby horses and for all other horses as well. (A very fast, very short workout will sharpen a horse's early speed and a long work that accents a quick beginning also may be useful, but only if the horse finishes in the same aggressive manner).

Each of the contenders for the 1985 Kentucky Derby reached the big race via every available route. Some raced often and worked sparingly, others followed a different training regimen.

Skywalker stopped racing a month before the race and worked four times, including a pair of mile workouts and two others at shorter distances.

Stephan's Odyssey ran in the Lexington Stakes on April 16 and had three workouts scheduled, including a mile on Monday of Derby week.

Spend a Buck set a record in the Garden State Stakes on April 20 and worked once on Wednesday of Derby week to match his previous winning pattern.

Eternal Prince, winner of the Wood Memorial, also was set into a relaxed working regimen, with a single 5-furlong work scheduled for Tuesday.

Proud Truth, Rhoman Rule and Tank's Prospect, all stretch runners who had their final Derby preps April 20, worked once at 5, 6 and 5 furlongs, respectively, on Sunday, Monday and Tuesday of Derby week, with both Rhoman Rule and Proud Truth working an additional 3 furlongs Friday, the day before the race.

Chief's Crown, who earned his role as the Derby favorite with a thoroughly professional win in the Blue Grass Stakes, worked 4 furlongs on a muddy track Wednesday of Derby week and appeared as sharp for the Derby as he was for his win in the Blue Grass Stakes.

In all this, there is a central point: To appreciate the subtleties of racing is to recognize the depth of the sport and to recognize the import of dozens of intriguing facts and factors as they influence the outcome of a single race. No one race or workout determines the outcome of a given race, but each workout, each piece of information may be a crucial clue toward the solution of a fascinating puzzle. That's handicapping, the joy of racing for millions of people from all walks of life.

No doubt the Kentucky Derby is the best-known race in the world and the most compelling, but for fans of the sport who have discovered the fun of handicapping, there is a challenge in every race and something to be learned every day.

# NOTES